Praise for *Boardroom Creativity*, How to Design the Future of Your Business

"*Boardroom Creativity* is a very useful guide when you know it's time for something different but you're not sure where to start. It gives a clear process and practical tools on how to design your future direction, leadership development, and even create your board."

Lino Tedeschi, Chairman and CEO of TESYA Group, Milan, Italy

"Boards are at the forefront of guiding organizational renewal to handle the unprecedented amount of change in the world. This book shares insights for how to approach innovation from board level and shows why you need to rethink your board work to stay future-proof."

Liselotte Engstam, Chair and Board Director, Researcher and Advisor, Stockholm, Sweden

"Business has been excessively focused on producing results, but it is always useful to go back to basics – people's contributions leveraged through excellent business processes generate excellent results. Furthermore, few authors recognize the importance of fair processes, particularly when it concerns creativity and innovation and when social and environmental contexts are important. This is a book for those looking for inspiration on creative business development that is also fair. I recommend it warmly."

Ludo Van der Heyden, INSEAD Chaired Professor Emeritus in Corporate Governance, Fontainebleau, France

"A timely message to change your business for the better. The authors' insights will propel your management teams to higher levels. The result is a clearer purpose, better focus, and m   ."

Guus Verhees, Impact Investor, M
SHIFT Invest, Randstad, The Nether

GW00568764

"I loved reading the book and am using it already. Today's complex business challenges require a creative approach that goes beyond brainstorming, and the examples and exercises inspired me to try out new ways of working."

Kerstin Stranimaier, Global Strategic Marketing Director of Huntsman Corporation, Basel, Switzerland

"Creativity is like energy or oxygen – you only realize how important it is when it's absent. *Boardroom Creativity* shows how to translate the abstract world of imagination and dreams into tangible realities. Creativity is what makes the progress of mankind possible."

Arash Aazami, Entrepreneur, System Innovator and Energy Transition Expert, Rotterdam, The Netherlands

"In order to innovate, business leaders should constantly learn and seek insight from diverse talents from both inside and outside the organization. Examples in the book demonstrate how powerful it is to bring creative people into the process when solving complex business challenges and developing the direction of your business."

Charlotte Møller-Andersen, Vice President Nordics & Benelux Zendesk, Copenhagen, Denmark

"Creative courage is essential for entrepreneurship – and it's a discipline – not a given. Applying these nine principles will help you to create remarkable opportunities."

Oscar Kneppers, Entrepreneur, Investor and Board Member, Amsterdam, The Netherlands

BOARDROOM CREATIVITY

How to
design
the future
of your
business

Fennemiek Gommer
Anne Mieke Eggenkamp

R^ethink

First published in Great Britain in 2022
by Rethink Press (www.rethinkpress.com)

© Copyright Fennemiek Gommer and Anne Mieke Eggenkamp
Authors photograph © Annaleen Louwes

To our dearest fellow travelers
Frederik, Karst, Ewout, Maarten

Contents

The road not taken

Two roads diverged in a yellow wood,
And sorry I could not travel both
And be one traveler, long I stood
And looked down one as far as I could
To where it bent in the undergrowth;

Then took the other, as just as fair,
And having perhaps the better claim,
Because it was grassy and wanted wear;
Though as for that the passing there
Had worn them really about the same.

And both that morning equally lay
In leaves no step had trodden black.
Oh, I kept the first for another day!
Yet knowing how way leads on to way,
I doubted if I should ever come back.

I shall be telling this with a sigh
Somewhere ages and ages hence:
Two roads diverged in a word, and I
I took the one less traveled by,
And that has made all the difference.

Robert Frost (1874–1963)

ENJOY
Introduction

"People rarely succeed unless they have fun in what they are doing."

Dale Carnegie[i]

Why this book?

The short answer is because we believe it's time to get serious about creativity. Our society needs more of it to find new solutions for today's complex challenges. We believe business can be changed for the better when leaders learn to embrace their creative intelligence. We've experienced that leadership teams are more successful at creating the future of their business when they approach it as a design challenge. Like the architect and inventor Buckminster Fuller said, "The best way to predict the future is to design it."[2] What would you like the future of your business to look like? Could you create new sources of income, build a more motivating place to work for your people, or redesign your business to be kinder to the planet? We invite you to use your imagination to take your business to the next level.

In the many years that we have partnered with leaders from different industries in various countries, we have seen that organizing business innovation as a design project works. First, because developing a new strategic direction calls for a different approach other than optimizing your current strategy as we'll show you in this book, and, second, because it's fun to do. If you enjoy what you're doing, you can be more successful as Dale Carnegie said. We've learned that when we design a process that is an enjoyable experience for all involved, it enables people to contribute, to learn and to own the outcome. Having fun improves the quality of the strategic output, and the resulting ownership is a prerequisite for successful transformation. Business innovation always requires cultural change, and innovation projects need to be designed for this from the start.

But we have also learned that something that comes so naturally to us – since both of us have been trained as designers – is less obvious for others. That's why we decided to write this book to share our learnings with people who are less familiar with applying creativity in a business context. We wrote it for leaders who feel it's time to transform their businesses to the next level, and who are curious to learn how to approach business innovation as a design project and develop their creative intelligence.

The joy of working together

We created this book as a duo because working together always makes us better and each of us brings a slightly different perspective. We share the same starting points: we both grew up as youngest daughters in entrepreneurial families. We were curious, creative and happy kids who were fortunate to have both left and right brain talents. And both of us chose a "path less traveled by," as the poem by Robert Frost so beautifully describes. We were the first to study design in our families, and we both ended up serving as board members, which is unusual for people with a creative background. We're innovators, eager to keep on learning, willing to understand different points of view and able to make unusual connections and look at problems and opportunities from multiple perspectives. We share a love for the unusual and combine future thinking with a passion for empowering people. We met when Anne Mieke was Chair of the Design Academy Eindhoven, and asked Fennemiek's consultancy to help her develop the strategic direction for this world-renowned design school. We quickly found out that we share an ambition to help people from different disciplines discover the potential of creativity, which eventually led to our business partnership and this book.

Fennemiek Gommer

Fennemiek is a creative thinker. She has written this book based on our shared principles which is why you'll read about "we" and "us." As a child, she wanted to be a creative writer and travel the world. Obtaining a Fulbright scholarship to study mathematics in the United States was a first step in realizing her international ambitions. The US academic system gave her the opportunity to also select creative classes such as photography, theater and writing. She graduated in industrial and product design in the Netherlands applying her analytic and creative brain, and quickly found that her strength was in conceptual thinking rather than in making. She complemented her studies with degrees in design thinking at the Domus Academy in Milan, brand strategy in the Netherlands, and the directors' program and innovation at INSEAD. Professionally, she grew up in SCAN Management Consultants: she joined in 1994 as a junior consultant, became managing partner after several years and left in 2004 to start her own consultancy with a business partner from the United Kingdom. She has always enjoyed complex business challenges, applying her creative problem-solving skills and international perspective to design different solutions. Being an "outsider," with one leg in the creative world and one in the business world, makes her a good connector of people and ideas. Growing up in a management consultancy made her realize that her design approach was different, starting from the desired end goal instead of analyzing (and potentially getting stuck) in the present. She's been a promotor of this future-led approach ever since, which also made her want to write this book. Fennemiek's specific expertise is in purpose-driven strategy and innovation, having worked as a consultant in those fields for more than 25 years.

Anne Mieke Eggenkamp

Anne Mieke is the creative maker of the two of us. She has designed this book and the illustrations in it with Fennemiek as her sparring partner. For as long as she can remember she has loved to draw, create new concepts and make things with her hands. Because of this, going to art school to study art and graphic design was an obvious choice even though she also excelled at sciences in high school. She's always been passionate about helping people grow, which led to a second degree in education. These interests came together after graduation when she started her own creative studio with a Canadian business partner. Together they pioneered digital design and taught designers how to use an Apple computer in the 1990s. In 2000, international interactive agency Razorfish recognized their frontrunner position and asked Anne Mieke to join. Her love for education brought her to the Design Academy Eindhoven (DAE) in 2006. In her role as Director of Education and Chair of the Executive Board she had the opportunity to co-create the future of the school with the students. She's passionate about the need to change the education system and feels we've been focusing too much on developing our left-brain skills and too little on stimulating our right-brain potential. Her TED Talk in 2013 was about "Acknowledging the creative: shifting the focus in education." This applies at primary school through to executive education and is a key reason for her desire to write this book. Since she left DAE ten years ago, she has been a promoter of the creative industry and creative leadership. Additionally, she has set up innovation labs for educational institutions and other organizations. Anne Mieke approaches innovation as a learning process. Her specific expertise is in leadership development and designing board room learning.

Together, we now lead Caracta Business Innovation, designing innovation journeys that result in new strategic directions and organizational change.

Learning from others

The future design challenge is unique for each company, and every leadership team will choose their own innovation journey – aiming for Robert Frost's "path less traveled by"[3] just like we did. But it always helps to learn from the experiences of those who have gone on the journey before. In this book, we share our insights from partnering with clients like AkzoNobel, SCA/Essity, Corbion, Atlassian and many others. Due to confidentiality reasons, we haven't always used the names of our clients.

The reasons to start our type of business innovation journey vary. We encourage you to read this book if your gut tells you that it's time to change your business direction, that you need a new approach and your team needs to learn how to become better at innovation. You may foresee your core offer becoming a commodity, the demand for your services declining or a new competitor disrupting the market. Or maybe you're experiencing problems attracting talented people for your team because their purpose and values are not aligned with your business culture.

It may also be you've worked with strategy consultants that were left-brain dominated in the past and have found that they provided you with a future direction but didn't empower the team to implement this new direction. Or you've always been happy working with them developing the strategy for your current business, but you were disappointed with their ideas for a new direction that didn't seem so new to you. Now you may be thinking that it is time to try something different, but you just aren't sure what "different" looks like yet. As we will show in this book, different to us does not mean outsourcing your strategy development to a different consultant, but designing a different type of process, learning to apply your right-brain using different tools and involving different people – both from inside and outside your organization.

In a process like this, you don't only learn from benchmarking other companies' innovation projects. Being creative, we find inspiration everywhere: in the people we work with, the books we read, the exhibitions we go to, our walks through nature and many other things. Some of the written sources of inspiration we share with you in this book. We're grateful to them for taking our thinking a step further and helping us to connect the dots. As Sir Isaac Newton, the famous English scientist, once said, "If I have seen further, it is by standing on the shoulders of giants."[4]

What we'd like you to learn

We have found that when business innovation fails in an organization, often there has not been a future-led approach, and there has been a lack of creativity in all aspects of the project. Sometimes the same people participated in workshops, and no outside experts or unusual suspects were invited, leading to more of the same instead of the breakthrough ideas needed. Other times the business transformation stalls because it has not been designed as a change process. Either too few people have been involved with little dialogue and no ownership at the end of the process, or there has been too little attention for building an innovation culture.

Once you have finished this book, we'd like you to see the advantage of approaching business innovation as a design challenge, know why you should get serious about creativity and understand how to apply our principles.

In our approach, the first set of four principles is:

1. **CREATE**: Innovation Is A Design Challenge.

2. **CHANGE**: It's Time To Transform.

3. **CARE**: Embrace Your True Purpose.

4. **LEARN**: Build Your Creative Confidence.

Together, they provide the foundation for our way of working and will show you that all of us are born with the imagination and creativity needed for business innovation.

The fifth principle forms a bridge between the first and second set:

5. **ACT**: Learn By Doing.

...leading on to the next set of four:

6. **ENGAGE**: Involve And Empower People.

7. **ENVISION**: Imagine A Better Future.

8. **EXPLORE**: Make It Happen.

9. **LEAD**: Redesign Your Board.

These principles will show you how to use your creative intelligence in a project to design the future of your business, and help you recognize that business innovation also requires board renewal. At the end of each chapter, we have added some questions for you to reflect upon. To facilitate applying the principles to your own business, you can download the workbook with the questions we introduce both in the illustrations and at the end of each chapter at www.caracta.com/book. We invite you to take some quiet time to think and consider each question and how it applies to where you currently are in your business. In the conclusion, we summarize the nine principles and encourage you to plan the next steps to future-proof your business.

Most of all, we hope you enjoy reading this book as much as we have enjoyed creating it.

PART ONE

THE FOUNDATION

1

CREATE

Innovation Is A Design Challenge

"Any corporation needs to do two basic things.
It must exploit what is and create what is not (yet)."

– Jonas Ridderstråle and Kjell Nordström[1]

Create what is not yet

The Greek philosopher Heraclitus famously said that change is the only constant in life.[2] The world is, and always has been, changing. Throughout the centuries, companies and people have adapted to those changes by learning new ways of doing things. To move forward, you need to be able to both exploit what is and create what is not yet. You may even have to completely redesign your future direction, your business model and the way you lead your organization.

This book focuses on the "create what is not yet" task of business. We like the quote at the beginning of this chapter because it's so obvious: all leaders agree that their company needs to both exploit and explore. The challenge is to make the time to explore and design the future. As one of our clients put it:

> "As the CEO of an international food group, I know I should be the one to make sure the company is prepared for the future, but the problem is that the complexity of today's business environment keeps me busy all day. Between dealing with the consequences of COVID, a potential cyber-attack and the war in the Ukraine, when do I allow myself the time to sit back and reflect?"

Living through the same circumstances as Chairs in our own boards, we more than understand this. You have no choice, though. If you don't spend time designing the future of your business, there will be no future. In this first chapter, we will explore how much time you should spend on business renewal and how to get the balance right between dealing with today's challenges and allowing time for innovation and development. We will help you understand when best to start your business innovation and, importantly, how to do this when you don't know what the future will bring.

While Heraclitus is right to say that change is nothing new to us, what is different today is the speed of change, especially in the field of technology. Accelerated change means shorter business cycles and a higher risk of being disrupted by competitors with new innovations based on new technologies, new offers and new business models. This means the balance between the energy you should spend on exploit versus explore shifts, while the need to spend more time on the future increases.

If you are like the CEO we quoted above, you intuitively know this, but you have a hard time bringing it into practice. What helps is to first agree with your team what the ideal balance should be for your business, as not all industries change at the same speed. Start from this desired balance (let's say it's 80% exploit to 20% explore, in your case), and map everything you do into those two categories to better understand your current situation.

When we did this with our client, it helped him decide what activities to stop to free up time and budget to prepare for the future. As he said:

> "I knew already that I was spending too much time on ongoing business, but to see the imbalance in front of me made me realize we needed to change our behavior. The first thing we did was to adjust the agenda of our board meetings, always allowing for time to discuss market developments, review innovation projects and visit relevant start-ups."

Do you know what the balance between exploit and explore is in your company? Do you invest enough in your "create what is not yet" tasks?

WHAT IS THE BALANCE BETWEEN "EXPLOIT" AND "EXPLORE" IN YOUR COMPANY?

EXPLOIT		EXPLORE
Executive	**Orientation**	Entrepreneurial
Control, focus, independence, and stability	**Dimensions**	Freedom, openness, collaboration, and flexibility
Cost, profit	**Strategic**	Innovation, growth
Utilize existing products, incremental innovation, optimize	**Business focus**	Explore new opportunities, breakthrough innovation, create
Low risks, margins, productivity, efficiency	**Management style**	Risk-taking, milestones, flexibility, effectivity
Minimal failure, control and monitor, predictability	**Culture**	Learning from failures, trial and error, rapid adaption
Linear execution, embracing planning, and productivity	**Processes**	Iterative experimentation, embracing creativity, and speed
Excel at organizing and planning, can design efficient processes to deliver on time and on budget, operational thinking, drive performance	**Leadership skills**	Excel in dealing with uncertainty, strong at pattern recognition, can navigate between big picture and details, adaptive thinking, encourage learning

These are the "exploit" and "explore" characteristics Anne Mieke has uncovered in her research for ScaleUpNation,[3] and that we have further developed based on the interviews we did for this book. We use it to discuss the current and desired balance between exploit/explore in our clients' businesses.

Design the future of your business

Everything alive, including business, has a lifecycle. Phases of rapid growth and maturity are followed by decline, whether you like it or not. Accelerated change results in a shortening of the corporate life expectancy. A study by Constellation Research shows that since 2000, 52% of companies in the Fortune 500 have either gone bankrupt, been acquired or ceased to exist because of digital disruption.[4] People's life expectancy has increased by 50% since 1950,[5] but a business's life expectancy has fallen by almost 500% in almost the same period. The average company lifespan on the S&P index was 61 years in 1958; it has now dropped to 18 years. This gives the old adage "Innovate or die" new meaning.

It also changes the nature of the innovation challenge. Besides developing new products and services, it is now also a more existential one of reinventing your business. Shorter life cycles lead to more fundamental business transformations.

We approach business transformation as a design challenge in which you design the future of your business, for example:

- "When all cars become smart, our business disappears. What will our future business look like?"

- "Disintermediation will happen sooner or later in our industry. What if we weren't a dealer anymore?"

- "Artificial Intelligence will take over part of our business. How can our people make the difference?"

Charles Handy has framed this business innovation imperative as the need to create a second curve.[6] Given the average lifespan of 18 years, we end up working with companies on their third, fourth or even fifth curve, sometimes even in parallel. The human challenge is that you should do this while you're still successful with your current cycle, and in fact haven't even reached the peak of your success yet. In this growth phase of business, we are all prone to being complacent.

It's a comfortable phase to be in, while the transition to a new curve comes with chaos and uncertainty.

How do you know it's time to design a second curve? You don't. It's easy in hindsight, but, looking forward, it's always a challenge to predict how fast trends will become reality. The first step in any change process is awareness. Have you discussed the concept of business life cycles with your team and where you are on the curve? It's good to be aware that our human biases tend to favor the status quo and that we generally underestimate the speed of change. Dealing with uncertainty means you need to be prepared for various scenarios and make room for experiments to explore what the second curve could look like. We advise you to free up time for creative sessions with your team, asking yourself the "what if?" questions:

- "What if we started a new business with the same purpose today – what would it look like?"

- "What if a new competitor entered the market – what unmet needs of our customers would they focus on? What could we do better that they would see as an opportunity to engage with our customers?"

- "What if robots could take over our services – what would be the human touch our clients would miss?"

- "What if this trend breaks through – what is the opportunity for us?"

Our food client now organizes yearly innovation labs in which a team of hand-picked young talent creates solutions to the design challenge, "What if our current business would cease to exist – what would our future business look like?"

We will describe how to do this starting from Chapter 5: ACT onwards.

WHERE WOULD YOU POSITION YOUR BUSINESS ON THE ORGANIZATIONAL LIFECYCLE?

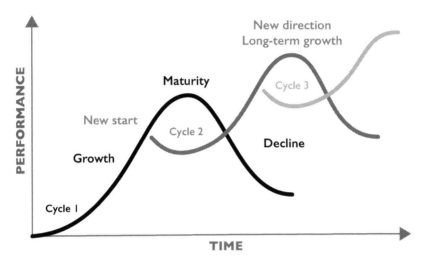

This illustration is based on Charles Handy's "second curve" principle. It shows that you should design your next future direction while you're still in the growth phase of the previous one. We ask our clients to position their own business on this curve.

Daring to sacrifice your current business

To stay future fit in today's fast changing world, you need to be flexible and change direction more often than before. As Charles Darwin wrote, "It's not the strongest of the species that survive, nor the most intelligent, but the one most responsive to change."[7]

In today's business environment, this has been labeled as agility. Agile companies think ahead, try to anticipate developments and adapt. Even for agile companies sensing what's going on in the world and understanding when it's time to create a second curve can be a challenge. Take Nokia, a textbook example of a company being able to re-invent itself, moving in and out of many different businesses such as paper, electricity and rubber galoshes. In the 1990s, they decided to focus on telecom and became the global market leader in mobile phones. They were the first company to develop a prototype of a touchscreen, internet-enabled phone at the end of the 1990s. However, they still managed to miss the major change in their market: the smartphone revolution that was caused by the introduction of the iPhone in 2007. At that time, Nokia was earning more than 50% of all their profits in the mobile-phone industry. They continued to focus on hardware instead of software, and between 2007 and 2012 lost $88 billion in market value. Their failure to adjust was caused by underestimating the importance of disruptive external trends, but there were also internal reasons. The Nokia leadership hesitated to invest in a new business direction that would potentially cannibalize the company's current products and services.[8]

This demonstrates a lack of creative courage many companies struggle with. American Express too wouldn't go into credit cards for a long time because it thought that this would cannibalize its Travelers Cheques business. Kodak is another classic example: it invented digital photography but had to file for bankruptcy in 2012 because it underestimated the fact that people were willing to compromise on technical quality for the sake of convenience.[9]

We're using well-known examples to illustrate this point, but most of our clients struggle with this. In hindsight, it's always easy to see where you took the wrong turn, but how can you know that the risk of sacrificing your current business will pay off? It's not a black and white decision. Like creative people, you can manage the risk by starting small, allowing yourself to experiment with pilot projects, or even setting up a separate business, as we will describe in Chapter 8: EXPLORE.

The bigger challenge is how to deal with not knowing what the future will bring. Renewal means venturing into the unknown and learning to deal with the fear and uncertainty that will always be part of this. It requires you to use your creative intelligence and let go of the need to be in control. Ed Catmull, President of Pixar Animation, describes management as a creative activity in his book *Creativity, Inc.*:

"I believe that managers must loosen their controls, not tighten them. They must accept risk; they must trust the people they work with and always pay attention to and engage with anything that creates fear. Moreover, successful leaders embrace the reality that their models may be wrong or incomplete. Only when we admit what we don't know can we ever hope to learn it."[10]

How do you deal with uncertainty? Do you dare to admit what you don't know? There is no innovation without uncertainty. To be uncertain is to be open to change, it enables you to question the status quo and explore new directions. Designers are taught to embrace a beginner's mindset; a mind that is willing to see everything as if for the first time. When you're certain of what you already know, it's hard to acquire new knowledge. Creative people are trying to discover their ignorance, not disguise it. They have the learning attitude that is needed for innovation, and we will cover more about this in Chapter 4: LEARN.

Creativity matters

Accelerated change increases the need for business innovation, and as a result the need for creativity increases as well. That creativity matters for future business success is a well-known fact. In the *Future of Jobs Report* of the World Economic Forum, creativity is listed as a top ten skill, moving from the tenth position in 2015 to the third position in 2020.[11] IBM's Global CEO Study, which surveyed 1,500 CEOs from 60 countries and 33 industries worldwide, concluded as early as 2010 that creativity was the most important leadership quality for success in business.[12] When asked about how to deal with uncertainty and complexity, many of the interviewed CEOs admitted that they felt overwhelmed by data while still being short on insight. They considered a better mastery of data analytics part of the solution, but at the same time realized they needed more creativity to act where certainty doesn't exist. They realized business model innovation needed to be done in the same way product designers keep improving their offerings based on ever-changing customer preferences, with disruptive competitive activity also driving business innovation. As the research report puts it, "The effect of rising complexity calls for CEOs and their teams to lead with bold creativity, connect with customers in imaginative ways and design their operations for speed and flexibility to position their organizations for twenty-first century success."

The most innovative CEOs in the IBM research saw the need to seed creativity across their organizations rather than set apart "creative types" in siloed departments like product design. To benefit from the diversity of ideas each employee can contribute, they encourage a new mindset of questioning. They invite employees at all levels to challenge assumptions based on past experiences and scrutinize "the way we've always done things."

Even though there are many advocates for the value of creativity in business today, there's still a lot of work to be done. In "Creativity has become the elephant in the board room," Jim Prior concludes that the real issue is not a lack of acknowledgment for the value of creativity but rather a lack in understanding how to apply it.[13] He quotes UK research that shows 96% of business leaders agree creativity is important in business strategy and 51% even believe it to be essential. However, 89% say that it is never discussed in board meetings, and 41% admit that no one is responsible for creativity in their business. It's a fundamental paradox: why don't business leaders make use of the quality that they indicate they need most?

Summary

In this chapter, we have introduced the first principle of CREATE. We have explored how you can achieve a balance between "exploit" and "explore" in your business, and looked at the phases of business growth and where your organization is on the business lifecycle curve.

Creativity matters in business because accelerated change requires increased innovation efforts which depend upon creativity. In our experience, the main hurdle is that creativity requires leaders to unlearn some of their current management practices, like doing thorough research before acting, and managing projects in a methodical and linear way. Business innovation requires learning to adapt new ways of thinking and doing, which we'll show in the second part of this book. Fortunately, everyone can learn to apply creativity to design the future of their business. In Chapter 4: LEARN, we write about how you can unleash the power of your own creative intelligence. As we'll see in the next chapter, CHANGE, the need for creativity in business will only increase further, making this question more and more urgent.

Reflection

Having read through this first principle, take a moment to consider the following questions:

- What is the situation like in your company?
- Do you recognize any "create what is not yet" business challenges?
- Does your team agree that creativity is important, and do you act accordingly?

2

CHANGE
It's Time To Transform

"The times they are a-changin'."

Bob Dylan[1]

Technology and humanity

Bob Dylan wrote "The Times They Are A-Changin'" in 1963, at the beginning of a decade that we now look back on as a period of political and social transformation. The Sixties movement started in the United States and United Kingdom but spread to continental Europe and other parts of the world. It was not just an era of change, but the change of an era – a major transformation just like the one we're experiencing today.

In this chapter, we will look at some of the key drivers of this change including climate change and the new technologies of the Fourth Industrial Revolution, or Industry 4.0. We'll also discuss how to deal with complex societal challenges such as globalization and digitization.

Klaus Schwab, Founder and Executive Chairman of the World Economic Forum, speaks about Industry 4.0 as a fusion of technologies that is blurring the lines between the physical, digital and biological spheres, and will change our lives at a speed that has no historical precedent. According to Schwab, "We stand on the brink of a technological revolution that will fundamentally alter the way we live, work, and relate to one another. In its scale, scope, and complexity, the transformation will be unlike anything humankind has experienced before."[2]

Since 2015, when Klaus Schwab first introduced the term to a wider audience, we've seen the notion that Industry 4.0 leads to digital transformation and the need for new business models become common knowledge. The systemic change he speaks of goes beyond digitization and calls for a holistic view. This has been recognized by the European Commission with their 2021 appeal for *Industry 5.0: Towards more sustainable, human-centric and resilient European industry*.[3] Instead of being technology-driven, Industry 5.0 is a value-driven approach to the technologies that are part of Industry 4.0. It recognizes the fact that transformation requires whole-brain intelligence: both left-brain (analytical/data driven and process-oriented thinking) and right-brain (creative and emotional intelligence). We'll describe this more in Chapter 4 when we discuss the principle of LEARN.

The new technologies of today's industrial revolution provide opportunities but also raise questions such as: can people change fast enough to keep up with technology? How do we redesign society to deal with the loss of current jobs? Can morality be programmed into AI? Andrew Keen, one of the world's best-known commentators on the digital revolution, urges us to recognize the dark side of the Internet such as the risks of data mining, intolerance, loss of respect for experts, growing inequality and the rise of narcissism.[4] We enjoy his thought-provoking talks because he goes beyond the critique and comes up with potential solutions for these issues. For his book **How to Fix the Future**, he interviewed people all over the world who are contributing to a better digital future through regulation, innovation, unleashing consumer power, stimulating citizenship and creating new education systems. His key argument is that technology requires us to stimulate humanity. Humans differ from machines through creativity, empathy and taking responsibility, and leaders and educators should bring out those qualities in people. It shouldn't be technology versus humanity (the title of another thought-provoking book on this topic by futurist Gerd Leonhard)[5], but technology and humanity.

How does your company respond to the technological revolution? Does your leadership stimulate human qualities such as creativity and empathy?

We can do better

Climate change is another key driver of change which takes us back to the 1960s, the age when environmental consciousness first started. In 1968, the Club of Rome was founded by Aurelio Peccei, an Italian industrialist, and Alexander King, the Scottish Head of Science at the Organisation for Economic Co-operation and Development (OECD). Their 1972 book *The Limits to Growth* has sold 30 million copies in more than 30 translations, making it the bestselling environmental book in world history.[6] A team of international researchers at the Massachusetts Institute of Technology (MIT) in Boston developed future scenarios based on five factors that they agreed determine (and ultimately limit) growth on this planet: population, agricultural production, non-renewable resource depletion, industrial output and pollution. Their key message: economic growth cannot continue indefinitely because of the limited availability of natural resources. From the start *The Limits to Growth* study created controversy, inspiring some to join the global sustainability movement and convincing others that there was no need to change their behaviors because there was not enough scientific proof.

Luckily, 50 years later, most of the leaders we work with see sustainability as the business imperative it should be. They embrace the concept of long-term value creation, aiming to optimize their triple bottom line of people, planet and profit. Their discussion on value creation goes beyond economic value and includes the ambition to create social and environmental value. We are happy to see that young people play a crucial role in putting sustainability on the agenda. Founders of start-ups include it in their purpose from the beginning, and in family-owned companies we notice the next generation of shareholders are often driving the debate. In other companies, future talents take the lead, or the children of the CEO indirectly influence the business direction. Since stopping climate change is still achievable but time is running short, we invite business leaders to take sustainability a step further. To have real impact, sustainability needs to be an integral part of your business strategy. Ultimately, it requires you to redesign the way you do business and redefine what growth means to you. We see sustainability as an opportunity for business innovation.

WHAT LONG TERM VALUE DO YOU WANT TO CREATE WITH YOUR BUSINESS?

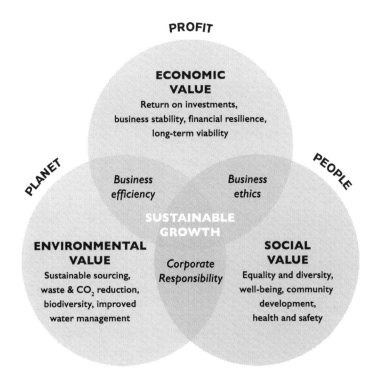

The Industry 5.0 goals are to create economic, social and environmental value. Some specific topics in each domain are listed above. Sometimes shareholders define what kind of value they wish to create; in other companies, the board takes the lead. The ambition needs to be clear before you start a business innovation journey.

Hearing the news about politics, education and so on, you could even argue that it's time to redesign our whole society. People's trust in government, business, media, and Non-Governmental Organizations (NGOs) is declining, as Edelman's Trust Barometer shows.[7] According to its research, the two essential elements of trust are effectiveness and ethical conduct, and our leaders and institutions are coming up short. Trust is declining overall, but slower for those that are higher educated. Business is becoming the only institution people feel they can trust. In most countries, businesses are now more trusted than the government. The result of all of this is that people expect business leaders to fill the void that is left by their governments and take the lead in realizing societal change. It's a call to action for business as former CEO of Patagonia Rose Marcario puts it:

> "Business as usual is not good enough anymore, and we want to lead by example. The plain truth is that capitalism needs to evolve if humanity is going to survive. More than ever, business needs to step up for democracy and a civil society."[8]

What if you saw this as an opportunity to redesign your business for the better? Could you improve your positive impact on society?

Complexity requires creativity

We realize that redesigning your business to improve your impact on people and planet is easier said than done. Climate change is a classic example of a so-called wicked problem, a term that was first introduced in 1973 by two Berkeley professors, Horst Rittel and Melvin Webber, to describe complex societal challenges such as terrorism, obesity and poverty.[9] A wicked problem has innumerable causes, is tough to describe and doesn't have one right answer. One of their key findings is that traditional processes can't resolve wicked problems; we need to find unconventional ways to address them. As John C. Camillus, a Professor of Strategic Management who wrote about wicked problems in strategy, notes:

> "Wicked problems are the opposite of hard but ordinary problems, which people can solve in a finite time period by applying standard techniques. Not only do conventional processes fail to tackle wicked problems, but they may exacerbate situations by generating undesirable consequences." [10]

Wicked problems are a business reality. Companies deal with increasing levels of complexity because of the consequences of globalization, digitization and escalating regulatory requirements. For example, the fact that a company needs to balance the needs of different stakeholders is nothing new, but, before, these stakeholders were represented by a few spokespersons of organizations such as trade unions. Today, each individual stakeholder can raise his or her voice via the social media. A famous example of this is the "United Breaks Guitars" video that Canadian musician Dave Carroll published on YouTube in July 2009.[11] It tells the story of how his guitar was broken by United Airlines baggage handlers, and the nine months of unsuccessful negotiations with the airline that followed. The song became an immediate hit upon its release and more than an embarrassment for United Airlines, who saw their stock price drop 10% within four days of the video being posted online.

As the above definition from John Camillus shows, wicked problems are the opposite of tame problems, and require a different approach. Tame problems are "right versus wrong" problems. At the end of the day there is a single "right" answer to be found. That doesn't mean tame problems are easy. They can be complicated to solve, but, like any type of puzzle, applying logic can provide the answer. Wicked problems, on the other hand, are "right vs. right" problems, with all sides claiming to be right. Wicked problems by nature can never be completely solved; there is no single best answer to the question. Potential solutions are somewhere on a scale between good and bad. Think, for example, of the challenge of how to deal with the COVID pandemic, or the question of whether you should withdraw your business from Russia to support the Ukraine. If so, how far do you go? Is China next because of how they treat the Uyghur people? One of our clients, who is active in these countries, said:

> "There are no easy answers on how to deal with the war in the Ukraine, even when you agree that ethics come first. Do we have more of a responsibility to take care of our people in the Ukraine than in Russia? Our team has different opinions on this. The important thing is to respect our differences and agree on our key values. From there we can create different solutions. We discuss our feelings about each option before we act on one of them, realizing we need to maybe change our course along the way. Sharing our own doubts from the beginning and keeping the lines of communication open during the whole process is crucial."

Dealing with this kind of complexity requires creativity: accepting that you don't have all the answers, daring to be vulnerable, understanding the needs of your stakeholders, and a willingness to try out different solutions and adapt when necessary. This means you need to practice your right brain skills, as we will see in Chapter 4: LEARN. How can you tell if your problem is a wicked one, so that you know you need to approach it in a more creative intelligent way than usual? The checklist in the illustration on the following page can help. Alternatively, we like the shortcut offered by Joseph C. Bentley, another business school professor who studied wicked problems:

> "Listen to the conversations, the debates, the arguments. Whenever there is more heat than light, more shouting than sharing, more anger than respect, you can be sure that the problem is wicked." [12]

Looking back, do you agree that traditional business processes don't solve wicked problems? Are you willing to try a different approach?

IS YOUR PROBLEM A TAME OR A WICKED ONE?

The more often you answer one of these questions with a yes, the higher the degree of wickedness involved in your problem.

Content complexity

☐ Do you have a hard time defining the problem? Does the problem definition change over time or seem vague to you? Or does the problem only become clear when you've tried to develop a solution?

☐ Is the information you have available ambiguous and incomplete? Or do different sources contradict each other?

☐ Can you identify several, interrelated causes to the problem? Or are the origins uncertain or unknown?

☐ Is it a problem that you have dealt with before with traditional problem-solving methods but that won't go away?

Social complexity

☐ Does the problem involve large numbers of stakeholders with different opinions?

☐ Is it difficult to formulate a clear end goal that all stakeholders share? Do the people involved have conflicting objectives?

☐ Do you feel your question potentially has different alternative solutions for different people involved?

☐ Is it less important to get to the "right answer" than to obtain the stakeholders' acceptance of the emerging solution?

Contextual complexity

☐ Do you need to deal with this problem in an environment of complexity, uncertainty, and fast change – both internally and externally?

☐ Are there many political and organizational issues involved?

☐ Do the solution constraints such as resources change over time?

☐ Does the issue relate to cultural values and are many different cultures involved?

Psychological complexity

☐ Are you taking a high personal risk when addressing this issue?

☐ Do you believe that you can't afford to be wrong because your actions will have a big impact?

☐ Is the answer to the problem linked to personal values and morals?

☐ Do you feel you need to make a trade-off in some way?

☐ Is an either/or choice involved?

We have created this checklist to determine whether you are dealing with a tame or a wicked problem because each demands a different approach. It is based on criteria developed by Hans Vermaak,[13] Rittel and Webber, and the interviews we did for this book.

Focus on the long term

The fact that sustainability is a wicked problem is not the only reason why it's difficult for business to become a force for good. Another challenge is the dominant focus on economic growth and shareholder value. As one of our clients, the CEO of a bank, told us:

> "There's a lot of talk about the triple bottom line, but profit always comes first. I can only invest in people and planet when my quarterly numbers stay on par with my competitors."

This is especially true for listed companies that follow the Anglo-Saxon model of governance that relies on the capital market, emphasizes the interests of shareholders and aims for profit maximization. French accountant Michel Albert was the first to contrast this model with what he called the Rhineland model, that is dominant in mainland Europe.[14] The main difference with the Anglo-Saxon model is that the Rhineland model looks at the interests of all stakeholders involved (shareholders, employees, customers, society and nature) and focuses on continuity rather than maximization of profits.

Unfortunately, the Anglo-Saxon model gained ground after the Second World War when American business schools and management literature became the standard for global business. In the Netherlands, for example, Rotterdam School of Management (RSM) research shows that in 1992, the subject of shareholder value figured prominently in the annual reports of only 13% of the Dutch top 100 listed companies; by 2006, it appeared in 74% of annual reports.[15] However, that same research shows that the emphasis on shareholder value is counterproductive because it negatively affects the long-term financial performance of those companies. This confirms the widespread criticism that the focus on shareholder value has led to short-termism in business and shows that focusing on the long-term creates economic value.

Luckily the tide is turning, and more and more CEOs have spoken up against the dogma of quarterly numbers, stressing the importance of balancing the short and the long term. Lou Gerstner, former CEO of IBM, would say in interviews that the preoccupation with short-term earnings in the public-company environment is a bad thing because it threatens longevity.[16] He questions if analysts have the long-term competitiveness of the company in mind, or whether they are focused too much on churning out numbers and wanting the earnings per share to go up every quarter. He summarizes, "The short-term pressure of analysts on current earnings can lead to underinvestment in the long-term competitiveness of a business."

It takes courage to ask shareholders to focus on long-term value creation, which is what Paul Polman, CEO of Unilever from 2009 to 2019, did.[17] In his *Unilever Sustainable Living Plan*, he set an ambitious vision to decouple business growth from its overall environmental footprint and increase the company's positive social impact. Besides introducing this ten-year plan, he also told his shareholders that they should no longer expect to see quarterly financial reports from the company, making it clear that he was looking for shareholders with a long-term perspective.

Today, more and more investors are embracing a long-term Environmental, Social and Governance (ESG) perspective, expecting companies to commit to ESG standards. In the future, ESG will become even more important because of integrated reporting. The Big Four accounting firms, together with the World Economic Forum and the International Business Council, have developed a set of ESG reporting metrics that do justice to the Rhineland model or what they call "stakeholder capitalism." [18] The pitfall of ESG metrics is that they are used for compliance. We see sustainability as an opportunity to redesign your business to create more long term economic, social and environmental value.

Summary

In this chapter, we have discussed the key challenges for businesses today – complex societal challenges, the climate crisis the world faces and the technological revolution that is affecting the way we live, work and interact with one another.

Like Paul Polman, mentioned earlier, we prefer long-term orientation in shareholders, which is why we enjoy working with family-owned companies and scale-ups backed by impact investors that share our purpose and values. You'll find more on the importance of shared purpose in the next chapter, CARE.

Reflection

Having read through this second principle, take a moment to consider the following questions:

- What major drivers of change might impact your business?

- How fast is your outside world changing?

- Do you wish to change your business for the better and create more economic, environmental and social value?

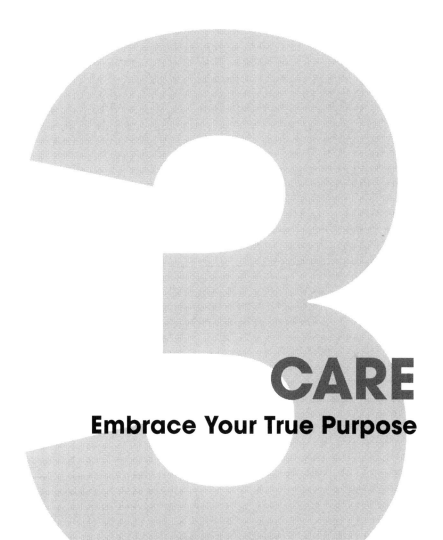

CARE
Embrace Your True Purpose

"Fight for the things that you care about but do it in a way that will lead others to join you."

Ruth Bader Ginsburg[1]

See the light

In Chapter 2: CHANGE, we wrote about the changes in the world that tell us it's time for business to transform. However, if your main driver for change is where you are on your business life cycle, incremental change could be sufficient. It's important to agree with your leadership team what type of change you're dealing with because change and transformation require a totally different approach.[2] In this chapter, we will look at the difference between change and transformation. We will explain how to recognize the differences between the two and discuss the approaches you might want to take. However, the key difference is that change is about improving the status quo starting from the now, while transformation starts with imagining a better future. This future-led approach is also how designers work, as we'll show in Chapter 7: ENVISION.

Change management deals with finite initiatives such as introducing a new performance management system, shifting from decentralized to centralized marketing support or developing new products. Transformation management deals with a portfolio of initiatives, which are interdependent or intersecting and designed to realize major shifts. The overall goal of transformation is to reinvent the company based on a vision for the future. It's much more unpredictable, iterative and experimental. For transformation, you need to get serious about creativity.

DOES YOUR BUSINESS INNOVATION CHALLENGE DEAL WITH CHANGE OR TRANSFORMATION?

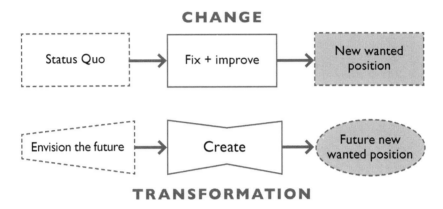

*As the illustration based on a **Harvard Business Review** article[2] on this topic shows, transformation requires a creative, future-led approach. This is the approach we describe in Part Three.*

What reason do you have to want to design your business for the better? All change starts with the motivation to do things differently. As the saying goes, "People either need to feel the pain or see the light." Some of our clients work with us because they feel the pain: their business is at the end of its lifecycle, disruptive new entrants force them to innovate or their customers demand it. However, most are intrinsically motivated to take their business to the next level. They've identified an exciting new market opportunity or want to have a more positive impact on society. The leaders we partner with fight for the things they care about, just like Ruth Bader Ginsberg, Supreme Court Justice and Women's Rights pioneer, suggests in her quote. The challenge is described in the second part of her quote: to do it in a way that others will follow. This is the reason why we recommend focusing on the opportunity that will motivate people to join the movement, whatever the original reason for transformation was. We encourage leaders to look for the people who want to change rather than those that feel they must change to create a guiding coalition to lead the way to the new future.[3] Others will follow.

Focusing on the positive is something we can learn from the cultural revolution in the '60s that we referred to in Chapter 2: CHANGE. There was plenty of pain in the '60s, with wicked problems related to racial segregation, the Vietnam War and women's rights, but for many there was hope. People could imagine a better future, aided not only by great new inventions such as the birth control pill, television and space technology, but also helped by their leaders who shared their dreams of a better future. Speeches from this decade are still used to inspire us today, such as John F. Kennedy's 1961 "We choose to go to the Moon" speech. In Martin Luther King, Jr.'s 1963 "I have a dream" speech, he recognizes the difficulties people face and references that according to the Declaration of Independence "all men are created equal."[4] His words moved people by inviting them to imagine a better future:

> "I have a dream that my four little children will one day live in a nation where they will not be judged by the color of their skin but by the content of their character."

Positivity is contagious, especially so when you are able to engage people on an emotional level and can help them visualize your dream in the way Martin Luther King, Jr. did.

What is your big dream? Which opportunities do you see to change your business for the better?

Create an innovation culture

To design new possible futures, you need a creative approach, including the ambition to change for the better and the ability to shift perspectives, make unusual connections and visualize what is not yet. Most of our clients will tell you that realizing their desired future was the bigger challenge. The managing partner of a law firm we partnered with told us afterwards:

"Once we had decided on our future direction, we felt that most of the work was done. We understood where we needed to go and thought we could just do it. We completely underestimated that we had to unlearn some of our existing practices, and how much time it takes to change an organizational culture. With hindsight, we should have put more effort into leadership development and organizational learning from the beginning."

Successful transformations require not only a new future direction but also adapting the new creative attitudes, behaviors and skills described in Chapter 4: LEARN. How do you create the culture of learning and innovation that transformation requires? It starts with identifying your true purpose.

The EY Beacon Institute partnered with Harvard Business Review Analytic Services to conduct a global survey across different sectors and geographies to investigate the business case for purpose. The survey defines organizational purpose as "an aspirational reason for being which inspires and provides a call to action for an organization and its partners and stakeholders and provides benefit to local and global society."[5] The report concludes that purpose is a powerful but underutilized asset. Their key findings are as follows:

- 89% of executives believed purpose matters as a driver for employee satisfaction, transformation ability and customer loyalty. Only 46% indicated their company has a strong sense of purpose.

- Executives from companies that treat purpose as a core driver of strategy and decision-making reported greater ability to drive successful innovation and transformational change. More than half (53%) of executives at companies with a strong sense of purpose said their organization is successful with innovation and transformation efforts, while less than one-fifth (19%) reported success at companies who have not thought about purpose.

This aligns with a benchmark study among leading innovators such as Pixar, Google and eBay that Harvard professor Linda Hill describes in her book **Collective Genius**.[6] Her research question was how leaders can build an organization that is capable of innovating continually over time. The companies she studied do this by creating a community that is both willing and able to innovate. To be willing, the community must share a sense of purpose, values and rules of engagement. To be able, companies must: identify opportunities and generate ideas through discourse and debate; experiment quickly, reflect and adjust; and make decisions that combine disparate and even opposing ideas. Identifying your true purpose is both the starting point for designing your new business direction and a prerequisite for creating an innovation culture.

DOES YOUR COMPANY HAVE A STRONG SENSE OF PURPOSE?

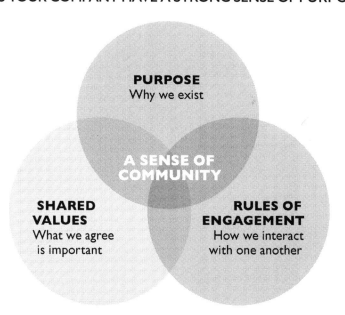

Harvard professor Linda Hill argues that building an innovation culture requires purpose, shared values and rules of engagement. Creativity in business starts with a common goal and clear boundaries.

Purpose-driven organizations are attractive places to work for, especially so for Millennials (born between 1981 and 1996) who will make up 75% of the workforce by 2025.[7] According to the Millennial Employee study, 64% of millennials won't accept a job when the employer doesn't have a strong corporate social responsibility policy. For Gen Z, the generation that is born after 1996, this is even more true. It's the first generation that prioritizes purpose over salary. They care deeply about the world around them, and they expect the company they work for to do the same and to be authentic about it. Attracting future talents requires you to be transparent about how your business is creating value beyond profitability.

When Fennemiek went on an inspiration journey to Silicon Valley to see what could be learned from companies such as Google, it was clear that the learnings went beyond technology and innovation. They were able to create the kind of purpose-driven innovation culture people from all over the world want to work for. As Steve Westly, venture capitalist, entrepreneur, politician and former board member of Tesla put it in his interview with Fennemiek:

> "I teach some of the smartest people of the world at the Stanford Graduate School of Business. They used to want to work for Goldman Sachs or McKinsey when they graduated, now they want to work for companies like Tesla, or start their own business and make a difference."

How to find your purpose and values

There are many ways to identify your purpose and values, and the scope of the effort varies from one session to a process of several months, depending also on how many people should participate. With the scale-ups we partner with, it's often a matter of one creative session with the founders. Even in bigger companies, it can be a leadership team exercise only. This provides speed but can also be a missed opportunity to create engagement and start the organizational learning journey. It's good to reflect before you begin if it makes sense to involve others, like asking family-members to participate in family-owned companies, engaging investors in scale-ups or involving young talents to ensure both a future perspective and motivate them. Inviting a fair representation of the company to take part in an intensive process, including different workshops with cross-functional teams, is especially relevant when you already know your organization's culture will need to change. You can than design the workshops and the creative tools in such a way that they kick-start the learning process. This kind of bottom-up process will give you input for both the current and desired values, but in the end the leadership team needs to decide which culture is needed for the transformation – keeping in mind that the gap can realistically be bridged. Values can be identified through dialogue, using creative tools or discussions on moral dilemmas.

For example, with the founders and management team of a break-through health innovation company, we used visuals to help uncover their talents and ambitions. Using drawings that we had prepared in advance, we asked each of the team members to pick three cards:

- One card to represent their personal talent.

- One card to illustrate what they perceive to be the key strength of the company.

- One card to visualize a strength that they would love to see more of in their company.

We then facilitated the discussion about their ambition for the future and what would continue to differentiate the company from their competitors. This brought them new insights, according to the founder:

"We had written our purpose around improving patients' lives, which in itself, of course, is a beautiful purpose that fits our industry and the needs of our end customers.

However, we're all techies: our passion is in product development and making the impossible happen. Our customers are business-to-business companies, and often we deal with tech people like us. Using the talent cards started our discussion in an unusual way and made us realize that staying on the forefront of technological developments was what would make us really happy – and how we could also be different from others."

Another method we use to support the development of a company's purpose are the primary purpose archetypes, introduced by Nikos Mourkaogiannis:

- **Discovery**: wanting to be the pioneer to do and discover new things. Examples include Sony, Intel and Virgin.

- **Altruism**: contributing to the common good. Examples include Wal-Mart, HP and BodyShop.

- **Excellence**: wanting to be the best. Examples include BMW, Berkshire Hathaway and Gillette.

- **Heroism**: being recognized by others for what you have achieved. Examples include Microsoft, Ford and ExxonMobil.[8]

When we use these archetypes, we select relevant examples from different industries to inspire the team to discuss their own purpose.

There are many creative tools you can use to kick-start a meaningful discussion. Most importantly, they need to work for you. It can be helpful to align with a framework that is familiar to your people. For example, some companies we partner with use Simon Sinek's "Golden Circle", or "why-how-what."[9] This model is easy to understand and became popular after his 2009 TED Talk, "How great leaders inspire action."

Whatever method you use, your business purpose needs to align with the personal purpose of your team to ensure it will be authentic and not just an advertising slogan – as the health innovation company example shows.

Purpose-driven brand positioning

We define brand positioning as follows:

> "Brand positioning refers to the conceptual place the company wants to own in the target audiences' minds, the essence of what the company wants to be known for."

It's your public promise. While it can be ambitious, it should be true enough to be credible. The whole organization needs to be aligned to living up to the brand promise. This includes not only your products and services, but also how you lead your people, address the press and engage with suppliers. When the health innovation company claimed to be at the forefront of technology, for example, it meant they needed to invest in their office space so that it felt more innovative.

Simon Sinek originally worked in advertising, and his "start with the why" framework originates from brand strategy theories. Brand gurus such as Kapferer[10] and Aaker[11] have been writing about the importance of looking beyond functional benefits and creating a brand that provides business direction and meaning since the 1990s, using companies such as Apple, Disney and IKEA as examples. When founded, the IKEA brand vision (their "why") was "to create a better everyday life for the many people," which is why they offered well-designed, functional home furnishing products at prices so low that as many people as possible would be able to afford them (their "what"). These are not just words on paper, but values to live by. Like founder Ingvar Kamprad used to say:

> "The IKEA spirit is a strong and living reality. I'm very proud to follow the rules of our company. If there is such a thing as good leadership, it is to give a good example. I have to do so for all the IKEA employees." [12]

While the idea of the brand strategy providing meaning and direction has been around for a while, what has changed is the thinking on how that brand should be developed. Where traditionally market-ers started outside-in by identifying the gaps in their market, now brand-owners are being challenged to start inside-out and develop purpose-driven brands. It goes beyond saying that you can only be successful when your customers feel you've added value to their lives. In the end it's not so much an either/or choice, but another example of and/and thinking. We help our clients develop a brand positioning that is both purpose-driven and based on insights from their audience using the model below. Ideally, we also find a hook into emerging consumer trends so that we can ride the undercurrent in society.

IKEA growth is helped by the fact that their promise was in line with a Swedish market development. In the late 1940s, when Ingvar Kamprad started advertising for IKEA in Sweden, the Social Democrats offered favorable loans to everyone who wanted to start a home. In the early 1970s, IKEA moved outside of Scandinavia and was able to surf the international trend of people wanting a lighter, more modern look rather than the traditional furniture of their ancestors.

DOES YOUR BRAND POSITIONING PROVIDE MEANING AND DIRECTION?

The Caracta framework to develop brand positioning starts from your strengths, matching them with customer insights and emerging trends.

When we helped Nyenrode reposition from "the Netherlands Business School" to "the spirit of enterprise" in 2005, these elements were all aligned. As Jacqueline van Marle, Marketing and Communication Director at the time, told us:

> "Nyenrode is the oldest private university of the Netherlands. It was founded in 1946 by a group of business entrepreneurs, led by Albert Plesman, aviation pioneer and the first Director of KLM. Entrepreneurship is in our DNA. When we speak to HR leaders they tell us they prefer Nyenrode graduates because of their 'can do' mentality. And the high school students who visit our campus are interested in Nyenrode because they want more than just theory (which is what they feel the academic universities offer). The challenge was that everbody in the team was a bit tired of this claim. That's why we were using other messages. Linking it to a new trend by showing us how we could benefit from the growing awareness of the role of intrapreneurship for innovation made the difference."

Does your brand promise align with who you are, and where you want to go? Could you adjust it in order to profit from emerging trends?

Summary

In this chapter, we have covered the important principle of CARE. We have looked at the difference between change and transformation and have shown you how to recognize which category your business challenge falls under. We explored the importance of creating a culture of innovation in your organization through developing a shared purpose and set of values, and we have explained some of our creative methods to help businesses find that shared purpose and value set.

Reflection

Having read through this third principle, take a moment to consider the following questions:

- Does your business have a purpose that goes beyond objectives?
- Is it providing direction for your future?
- Are you building your innovation culture on the foundation of shared purpose and values?

4

LEARN

Build Your Creative Confidence

"The world as we have created it is a process of our thinking.
It cannot be changed without changing our thinking."

Albert Einstein[1]

Creativity can be learned

Albert Einstein, arguably one of the smartest men ever, is often quoted by designers because of his belief in creativity. He said things such as, "The true sign of intelligence is imagination and not knowledge," and encouraged people to be curious, playful and non-conformist. He believed that problems cannot be solved with the same thinking that was used to create them. In other words, when you want to transform your business, you first need to change the way you think.

Like Einstein, we encourage the leaders we partner with to develop their creative intelligence. However, when we start working with them, they often tell us that creativity is a matter of talent and not something they will be able to learn.

How about you? Do you think you can learn to be more creative? In this chapter, we will explore how past experiences have impacted people's creativity. We will look at the need to change how you think if you want to change your business. A growth mindset will nourish your creativity. We will discuss how learning helps leaders become the best they can be and how their leadership style can enable them to exploit and explore new opportunities to grow their business.

You may be surprised by the research findings of INSEAD professor Nathan Furr, who looked at the balance between nature and nurture for both IQ (general intelligence) and CQ (creative intelligence).[2]

The results show that while IQ is roughly 80% genetic, only approximately 33% of CQ is genetic. Creativity and innovative leadership are qualities we develop, not qualities we are born with. When Anne Mieke was the Chair of the Eindhoven Design Academy, she witnessed the big leaps people made in becoming more creative and learning how to apply their creative intelligence in the different phases of the design process. Together with her team, she made this happen by carefully designing the learning programs to fit both personal development objectives and project objectives, intertwining them as the warp and weft of a fabric.

The fact that only 33% of creativity is in your genes also shows the importance of having a growth mindset, a concept that was first introduced by psychologist Carol Dweck from Stanford University.[3] People with a growth mindset believe that they can improve their intelligence through effort and learning, in contrast to people with a fixed mindset who believe their intelligence is fixed and static. When you have a growth mindset, you understand that not knowing or not being good at something can be a temporary state, so you're not afraid to try again. Creative people share many of the same characteristics that are part of having a growth mindset. Noticeable examples are curiosity, being optimistic, seeking the opportunity in a challenge, and having the courage to take risks and try out new things. As we will see later, entrepreneurs also share those same characteristics. When business leaders associate creativity with making art, we invite them to develop their entrepreneurial mindset instead.

We see innovation as a learning journey, and the willingness to learn as a key success factor for business innovation journeys. Did you know that only one out of four business transformations succeeds?[4] As we showed in Chapter 1: CREATE, the challenge is often a human one, having to overcome biases such as a preference for the status quo. Another bias we frequently encounter in the boardroom is

WHAT KIND OF MINDSET DO YOU HAVE?

FIXED ➡ **GROWTH**

- Avoids challenges
- Gives up easily
- Sees effort as pointless
- Ignores useful negative feedback
- Feels threatened by
  the success of others

- Embraces challenges
- Persists in the face of setbacks
- Sees effort as a path to mastery
- Learns from criticism
- Finds inspiration and learnings
  in the success of others

We made this summary based on the work by Carol Dweck, who introduced the concept of growth mindset. We believe this is the attitude you need to develop to become more creative and lead business innovation.

the overconfidence bias, which is a hurdle for learning. As philosopher Eric Hoffer says, "To learn, you need a certain degree of confidence – not too much, not too little. If you have too little confidence, you'll think you can't learn. If you have too much, you'll think you don't have to learn."[5]

Are you open to learn to become more creative?

Using left-brain/right-brain as a metaphor

Ned Herrmann's Brain Dominance Instrument (HBDI) introduces four quadrants that represent different brain orientations with specific strengths and skills.[6] The upper part is more geared towards thinking (analytical and creative), while the lower part is more geared towards acting (operational and social). The beauty of this tool is that Ned Herrmann already developed it in 1976, when he was Head of Management Education at General Electric. Since then, countless individuals have been plotted, so we now know the average HBDI profiles for different organizations and occupational functions.

It probably won't surprise you that most multinationals, executives and management consultants have a more "exploit" leadership profile: high on analytical and operational (left-brain), low on creativity and social (right-brain), while creative agencies, entrepreneurs and designers often have a dominant "explore" (right-brain) orientation. Stereotypically, left-brain people like being in control and knowing what will happen next, while right-brain people prefer the adventure of the unexpected. This explains why scale-ups and other companies that are led by entrepreneurs are often better at dealing with uncertainty and complexity. Left-brain dominated companies prefer sequential processes, while the nonlinear approach to business innovation that we describe in Chapter 5: ACT comes more natural to companies that are predominantly right-brain.

WHICH THINKING STYLE DO YOU PREFER?

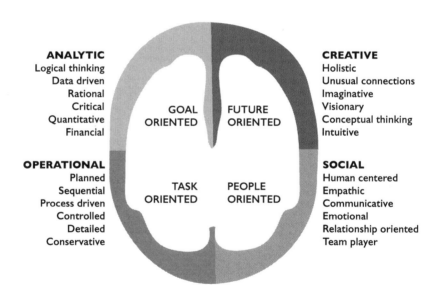

ANALYTIC
Logical thinking
Data driven
Rational
Critical
Quantitative
Financial

GOAL
ORIENTED

FUTURE
ORIENTED

CREATIVE
Holistic
Unusual connections
Imaginative
Visionary
Conceptual thinking
Intuitive

OPERATIONAL
Planned
Sequential
Process driven
Controlled
Detailed
Conservative

TASK
ORIENTED

PEOPLE
ORIENTED

SOCIAL
Human centered
Empathic
Communicative
Emotional
Relationship oriented
Team player

Ned Herrmann researched the dominant thinking styles in different organizations and occupational functions, and concluded that managers often have a left-brain dominance, while entrepreneurs have a right-brain dominance. Business innovation requires you to develop your right-brain competencies.

We're using Ned Herrmann's left-brain/right-brain metaphor because it's easily understood, but like all models it has its limitations. It's a human construct to make sense of reality and not a true representation of reality. In the past decades, neuroscience has understood more and more about how the brain works. Recent research by Professor Hikaru Takeuchi confirms that the brains of creative people are different.[7] This is not because one half is more developed than the other, but because creative people have more white matter than others. We find this very interesting, because white matter is the connective tissue between the gray matter, which usually depicts the brain and houses all knowledge. The fact that creative people have more white matter makes them better at associating and connecting old ideas in new combinations. According to Apple Founder Steve Jobs:

> "Creativity is just connecting things. When you ask creative people how they did something, they feel a little guilty because they didn't really do it, they just saw something. It seemed obvious to them after a while. That's because they were able to connect experiences they've had and synthesize new things."[8]

We like this quote not only because Steve Jobs talks about the creative ability of being able to connect different experiences, but also because he talks about creative people "just seeing something." Observation is the foundation for creative thinking. You observe with all your senses: hearing, seeing, feeling, smelling and tasting. Often you do this unconsciously, but you can train yourself to do it more consciously. The more diverse experiences you have, the more dots you can connect and the better your creative problem-solving will be. Takeuchi's research confirms this and also supports our strong belief that everyone can learn to be more creative. People can grow more white tissue.

Even though in reality creative people use their whole brain, we continue to refer to the left-brain/right-brain metaphor. It helps to explain the different leadership styles and associated mindset and skills.

Leaders are learners

In Chapter I: CREATE, we wrote about the need for companies to exploit what is and explore what is not yet at the same time. Exploit and explore require different leaderships styles – executive leadership for exploit and entrepreneurial leadership for explore.

Executive leaders emphasize exploitation over exploration when setting their strategic priorities. Their focus is on getting things done and getting results. They excel at implementing the existing strategy and optimizing the existing business. Executive leaders tend to prefer their left-brain thinking styles.

For entrepreneurial leaders, it's the other way around. They emphasize exploration over exploitation. Their focus is on creating new business opportunities, rejuvenating the organization by getting people to challenge the existing business model and stimulating innovation. Entrepreneurial leaders tend to favor their right-brain qualities.

The combination of both styles of leadership is called ambidextrous leadership. Ambidexterity means the ability to use both the right and left hand equally well; in leadership it refers to the ability to innovate (explore) while operating the existing business (exploit) effectively and efficiently. Ambidexterity invites you to embrace the concept of both/and, rather than either/or. The right balance between executive and entrepreneurial leadership depends on your business situation, but in general the need to focus more on explore is increasing in a fast-changing world. While any company needs both types of abilities to be successful, we rarely meet leaders who are successful at doing both. Therefore, we encourage our clients to create ambidextrous teams. What is the right mix for your business?

Transformation requires you to redesign your leadership team to fit the future of your business. We'll write more about this in Chapter 9: LEAD.

WHERE ARE YOU ON THE SCALE OF EXECUTIVE VERSUS ENTREPRENEURIAL LEADERSHIP?

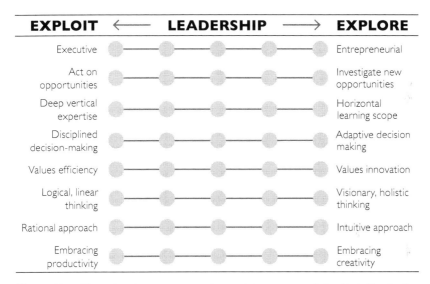

EXPLOIT	←	LEADERSHIP	→	EXPLORE
Executive				Entrepreneurial
Act on opportunities				Investigate new opportunities
Deep vertical expertise				Horizontal learning scope
Disciplined decision-making				Adaptive decision making
Values efficiency				Values innovation
Logical, linear thinking				Visionary, holistic thinking
Rational approach				Intuitive approach
Embracing productivity				Embracing creativity

We use this tool in our learning programs to raise people's awareness of what kind of leader they are and to stimulate an open dialogue on what the team needs to develop.

Sometimes the right balance between executive and entrepreneurial leadership is a matter of changing the composition of your team. Other times you can design leadership development programs to help your team develop new mindsets and skills. For start-ups, for example, the next growth phase to become a scale-up demands a different leadership style. The founder gets a new role or an outside CEO comes in. This is a moment when the leadership team needs extra support. As one of our clients, the founder of a tech-fashion scale-up, described it:

"As typical entrepreneurs, we cherished our freedom and were proud of our ability to change direction every day. Working with you made us realize that our next growth phase required something different from us: that we needed to safeguard our creativity and speed, but at the same time increase our productivity and scale. It meant that we needed to develop a better-defined strategy and shift our focus from predominantly product development to a more commercial orientation. The most difficult part was that we needed to change the culture from an informal one to clear structure and processes. That was a real challenge. For us, structure meant control and loss of our freedom. You helped us find the right balance and showed us how to build a culture of continuous experimentation and learning."

Adapting to a changing world means changing the team composition as well as a willingness to never stop learning. In our opinion, the best leaders are learners. They are open to incorporating new behaviors themselves and can mobilize others in their organization to do the same. Learning programs should be specifically designed to realize the business transformation needed. While many scale-ups need to strengthen their executive leadership style, most established companies ask us to further develop their entrepreneurial leadership capabilities. Entrepreneurial leaders are good at experimenting, learning and iterating – a prerequisite for leading a business innovation journey, as you will see in the second set of principles starting with ACT (which you will read about in Chapter 5). This is the kind of leadership style you can develop by training your creative muscle.

Creativity is a muscle

In our Boardroom Oxygen programs that help unleash the creative intelligence of leadership teams, we ask leaders to first do a self-assessment of their own creativity. They often hesitate to do so because of their misconception that being creative is related to being an artist. You can be very creative and never touch a paintbrush or sing a note. Children are born creative but lose their creativity as they transition through life and into adulthood. Since the First Industrial Revolution, we have valued our left-brain competencies the most – both in education and business – as Ken Robinson so eloquently explains in the most watched TEDx Talk ever, "How schools kill creativity."[9] While the focus on analysis and process helped advance western economy for a long time, it's not enough in today's world. Traditionally, creative education is related to being artistic. We're taught how to draw, but also how to self-judge that our drawing is not good enough. "I cannot draw" is one of the first things our clients say when we ask them to visualize what good looks like – even when we use other creative tools. One of our favorite writers, Brené Brown, calls these "creativity scars people collect."[10] In her shame research, she found that 85% of people could recall a school incident from their childhood that was so shaming that it changed how they thought about themselves as learners. What impressed her, and why she came up with the concept of "creativity scars," is that about half of those memories were related to creative activities:

> "The research participants could point to a specific incident where they were told or shown that they weren't good writers, artists, musicians, dancers, or something creative. This helps explain why the gremlins are so powerful when it comes to creativity and innovation."

We urge you to ignore your gremlins and believe in your creative abilities despite those scars. Creativity is like a muscle: you can train it to regain your creative confidence and learn how to apply it. Like any muscle, creativity needs nourishment. What that looks like is different for everybody. It doesn't matter what you do, so long as it fills the creative well for you. You may get your inspiration from going to museums, theaters and movies, or from learning new things, reading, playing, cooking or inspiring conversations. It can be anything you enjoy that stimulates your curiosity and your senses. Ample nourishment is the foundation for the further development of your creative competencies. As fashion designer Paul Smith puts it:

> **"You can find inspiration in everything. If you can't, then you're not looking properly."** [11]

Here are some of our favorite creative habits that you may want to experiment with, but there are many others:

- You can develop your intuition by taking short breaks in your business day (to take a walk, listen to music or reflect) and paying attention to the ideas that come up. Make sure to stop and capture those intuitive insights in a (digital) notebook.

- To stimulate new ideas, change your networking habits. Instead of reaching out to your usual business contacts, why don't you also plan time to meet people that are outside your regular network? You can also use this to experiment with stepping out of your comfort zone or to practice empathy.

- Empathy can be trained by being intentionally curious about people all day, asking questions, and avoiding "I" statements and talking about yourself. You can set yourself a target to reduce your airtime to $1/3$ of the total time, keeping in mind the saying that it's not for nothing people have two ears and one mouth. Listening is a key people skill.

- Another key creative skill – connecting the dots between seemingly unrelated concepts – can be developed by using more metaphors. This is something you can practice in your regular business presentations as well as at dinner parties with your friends. What metaphor would you use to describe your business objective, last vacation or a book you just read?

Like all creative journeys, this is an iterative process. Start small, pick a creative habit that appeals to you and, once it has become second nature, you can try another one.

Summary

In this chapter, we have covered how creativity can be learned if you develop a growth mindset. We've discussed how to develop that creativity for the benefit of your business and how your leadership style can help to create new business opportunities. Leaders are learners, and business innovation is something you learn by doing as we'll see in the next chapter, ACT.

Reflection

Having read through this fourth principle, take a moment to consider the following questions:

- What kind of leader do you want to be?
- Do you have a growth mindset?
- Is developing creative intelligence relevant for your business?

PART TWO

THE BRIDGE

ACT

Learn By Doing

"The most difficult thing is the decision
to act. The rest is merely tenacity."

Amelia Earhart[1]

Business innovation is a journey

How do you design new possible futures for your business? That is what the next chapters – ENGAGE, ENVISION and EXPLORE – will focus on. And when do you start? When you're ready to take your business to the next level, as we've explained in Chapter 2: CHANGE. You can wait until you're nearing the peak of your current business model and it's time to design a second curve, but how do you decide when the time is right? As Amelia Earhart, the first female aviator to fly solo across the Atlantic Ocean, says, "The most difficult thing is the decision to act."

In this chapter, we will discuss how to make innovation an everyday part of your business. We will look at how you plan the roadmap to take you on your journey. We'll show you our approach to business innovation and how it differs from traditional strategy development to effectively deal with the uncertainty the future brings. We will also highlight pitfalls that will prevent successful implementation of changes.

Let's start with how to create a culture of innovation. We advise you to make creating the future part of your ongoing business by regularly setting aside time for "what if?" sessions to stimulate a culture of innovation. This way you can either adapt your current business direction or introduce a new one when needed. Once you've envisioned what you want your business to be like in the future, we encourage you to create a roadmap that will guide you there instead of a detailed operational plan. A roadmap outlining the big shifts needed to transform your business enables you to adjust to the opportunities and threats that our fast-changing world provides. It also means the board needs to make sure their leaders are able to sense what's going on in the world and pivot when necessary, as we'll describe in the final chapter of this book, LEAD.

We approach business innovation as an ongoing journey, starting with the following phases:

- The ENGAGE phase is about connecting to the people inside and outside your company. People make the difference between an average result and a great one. For which customers do you want to create value? What are their unmet needs? How can other stakeholders help or hinder the transformation? Whom should we involve for their expertise, creative solutions or buy-in?

- In the ENVISION phase, you use your imagination to answer the questions: What do we want our business to look like in the future? How can we bring our purpose to life in different ways? What big opportunities do we see?

- Finally, in the EXPLORE phase, you map the consequences of the possible future directions and identify which key business and leadership shifts are needed to turn the vision into a reality. You set up experiments to be able to stress-test and improve your ideas.

In theory, the EXPLORE phase, with its focus on continuous improvement, could go on until it's time to design the next curve with a new future for your business, as we've shown in CREATE.

WHICH PHASE OF THE INNOVATION JOURNEY ARE YOU IN?

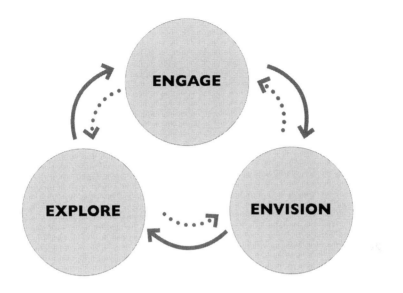

Every innovation journey starts with engaging people inside and outside the company, involving them in envisioning new possible futures and exploring what transformation is needed to realize the desired future.

A common pitfall we see is that leaders don't pay enough attention to the ENGAGE phase and start their project with developing a vision of the future. Designing the team and the process before you start is crucial. Business innovation always requires transformation, and the project should be designed as a change process: identifying who will lead the change, involving the change agents and approaching the process as a learning journey. Doing so heightens your chances of a successful implementation.

The pitfall of not involving the right people also applies to the ENVISION phase. Developing a vision of the future is the responsibility of the business leader, but it can be done in different ways. A common misperception is that the vision should be developed by a single visionary leader, charismatic men like Jack Welch, former

CEO of GE, who said, "Good business leaders create a vision, articulate the vision, passionately own the vision, and relentlessly drive it to completion." [2]

In practice, envisioning is a collaborative effort. In the words of Professor Herminia Ibarra, expert in leadership and learning:

> "Visionary leaders don't have to answer the question 'Where are we going?' all by themselves. As they search for new paths, they conduct a vigorous exchange with an array of people inside and outside their organizations, knowing that great visions rarely emerge from solitary analysis." [3]

Who are the people you would like to take along on your innovation journey? What expertise do you need, and who dares to challenge your ideas of the world?

Design is an iterative process

In a traditional project management approach, you complete a project within a linear sequence. You plan the different steps from A to B, execute, finish and evaluate. The scope of the project is defined at the beginning, with clear expectations, responsibilities and stage-gates to decide when to go to the next step. For designers, the road from A to B is not a linear one but an iterative one. They learn by doing, experimenting, failing and adjusting along the way – just like entrepreneurs do. This also means the three design phases won't always happen in the order that we illustrated above. You may be setting up a pilot in the EXPLORE phase and realize that you need more customer insights (back to ENGAGE) or a different vision of the future (ENVISION). A design process is a messy process, circling back and forth but moving forwards nonetheless. It takes creative courage to keep on trying, even when your previous attempt has failed and you're not sure what's next.

WHAT ARE THE KEY DIFFERENCES BETWEEN A LINEAR AND AN ITERATIVE PROCESS?

LINEAR PROCESS	ITERATIVE PROCESS
Straight from A to B	In cycles from A to B
Process first	People first
Focus on end deliverables	Multiple in between deliverables
Project management methods	Agile ways of working
Requirements remain unchanged	Requirements will change
Stakeholder engagement at start and implementation	Stakeholder engagement during the whole process
Knowing and doing	Failing and adjusting
Evaluate and learn when finished	Learn by doing and feedback loops
Tasks and milestones	Experiments and adjustments

Wicked challenges, like designing the future of your business, need to be addressed with an iterative process. An iterative, or agile, process differs from a linear one in many ways. The key characteristics of both approaches are listed above.

The courage to try out new things is often associated with having a high risk-appetite. Richard Branson mentions in interviews that being daring made him successful:

> "Saying yes is a lot more fun than saying no. It's gotten me into a lot of trouble, and certainly nearly killed me on many occasions. But if I didn't have that spirit in me, Virgin wouldn't be a global brand."[4]

The entrepreneur's willingness to take risks is confirmed by various studies. For example, recent research on the key differences between entrepreneurs, CEOs and employees concluded that entrepreneurs showed the greatest tolerance of risk combined with the strongest belief in their ability to succeed in challenging situations.[5]

We don't feel the stereotype of "high risk-takers" does justice to entrepreneurs. Entrepreneurial success starts with identifying an exciting business opportunity, not with identifying a worthy risk. It's the tolerance of the risk that comes with the opportunity that makes the difference. Having the courage to accept those risks is a prerequisite for growth, though. And by the way, the entrepreneurial leaders we work with aren't willing to go as far as risking their lives like Richard Branson does. In Chapter 8: EXPLORE, we'll show you how to take calculated risks by starting out small with pilots. Just like the prototypes of designers, these smaller sized experiments are designed to fail quickly and cheaply.

A key objective of an iterative, or agile, process is to introduce something tangible as quickly as possible, so you can collect feedback and improve the next version. We did it with this book as well, first sending out a so-called beta version to collect input from some of the people we respect. The book is much better thanks to their input. In software development this is called launching a Minimum Viable Product (MVP), a term that became popular thanks to the success of the "lean startup" movement by Eric Ries.[6] Instead of spending years perfecting your new product or service, you launch an MVP, secure your first customers, collect feedback and change the product regularly – launching new versions when they are ready.

You can imagine that this way of working requires a different type of mindset than the traditional "let's first make sure it's perfect" approach. Business innovation processes require creative thinking and doing from the beginning to the end.

Creativity all the way

Everyone will tell you that innovation requires creativity, but often we see it being used only in brainstorm sessions to come up with new ideas and solutions. This focus on idea development can also be found in Professor Robert Franken's definition of creativity in his book *Human Motivation*. He writes, "Creativity is the tendency to generate or recognize ideas, alternatives, or possibilities that may be useful in solving problems, communicating with others, and entertaining ourselves and others."[7]

The focus on idea development is especially true for product and service innovation. In business strategy, we notice people use creative tools even less – not even for ideation.

Creative thinking can be encouraged in brainstorm sessions with all sorts of creative exercises, techniques and tools. Provided there is a clear structure with an agenda that is designed for the specific challenge, tools are selected that will lead to the desired outcome and you have a location that inspires creativity, you can achieve great results. There are many different courses, creative facilitators and workbooks that you can use to support you in this. One of our favorite creative manuals is **ThinkerToys** by former US Army Officer Michael Michalko.[8] Michalko organized a team of NATO intelligence specialists and international academics to research, collect and categorize all known inventive-thinking methods. His team applied these methods to various NATO military, political and social problems, resulting in a variety of creative solutions to new and old problems. The **ThinkerToys** workbook provides an overview of techniques that you can use to either develop your own creative thinking or to inspire ideation in creative sessions. "Idea Quota," for example, is an exercise where for a week you challenge yourself to come up with five new ideas on an issue you are working on. It stretches the mind and forces you to begin thinking of different possibilities. You can pick and choose the ones that speak to you personally and fit your business challenge.

Alex Faickney Osborn, the "O" of the advertising agency BBDO, is the one who came up with the term "brainstorming" in 1942.[9] We used one of his creative tools, the SCAMPER method, when we helped the leadership team of a library develop their future direction.

SCAMPER stands for:

- **S – Substitute something**: Instead of lending books, I could do... to encourage more people to read.

- **C – Combine it with something else**: If we would combine... with our core function of books, we could attract more visitors to the library.

- **A – Adapt something to it**: If we look at libraries in other countries, we could adapt... to create a better experience.

- **M – Modify or Magnify it**: What can we emphasize even more to make our proposition future-proof?

- **P – Put it to some other use**: We have a building; what else can we use it for?

- **E – Eliminate something**: If we get rid of the building, we can still provide the same experience by...

- **R – Reverse or Rearrange it**: If we would re-arrange the subscription process, what would it look like?

These are just a few of the questions we used in the process. The main objective of the SCAMPER exercise is to look at a challenge from different angles. As the project leader of the library said afterwards:

"In our previous strategy development project, we started from our objective of attracting more users and developed a plan to achieve this – mainly by increasing our marketing efforts. Using the SCAMPER method forced us to look at our questions from different perspectives, which enabled us to come up with a more creative, holistic approach."

While creativity is standard practice in innovation, the pitfall is to use it exclusively for coming up with new ideas. Brainstorming, or creative thinking, is not the only part of the innovation journey where creativity matters. In his book *Creativity*, Professor Mihaly Csikszentmihalyi's also includes creative doing. He writes, "Creativity is any act, idea, or product that changes an existing domain, or that transforms an existing domain into a new one…" [10]

We encourage you to apply your creative intelligence to the whole business innovation process as illustrated here: from sensing the undercurrents in society to relating to your stakeholders and from designing future directions to creating prototypes. We'll show you how to do this in ENGAGE, ENVISION and EXPLORE.

DO YOU APPLY CREATIVITY IN ALL PHASES OF THE BUSINESS INNOVATION JOURNEY?

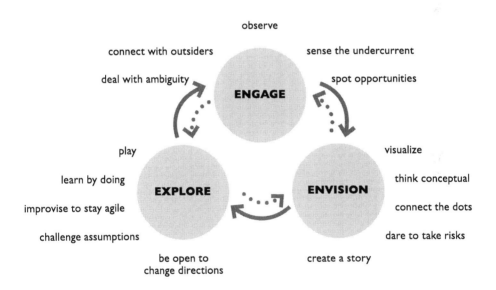

We believe in the value of applying creativity in the whole business innovation journey. We often only see it being used for brainstorming and ideation. The illustration shows the core creative skills to be applied per phase.

Why fair process matters

Creating an environment where people can trust each other is a prerequisite for individual team members to dare to unleash their creativity, reflect on their actions and be open to learn. We believe trust is built on the foundation of fairness. When it comes to fairness, one of our sources of inspiration is Professor Ludo Van der Heyden, Founder of INSEAD's Corporate Governance Center, and leader of the International Directors Programme at the time that Fennemiek participated in this thought-provoking course. Ludo Van der Heyden is a great advocate of what he calls Fair Process Leadership, a concept that strongly resonates with us because of its human-centric and value-based approach.[11] He argues that fair business practices increase both performance and sustainability. His emphasis is on fair play and not fair share. A fair process typically results in outcomes that are considered fair as those concerned and affected will be engaged in framing the challenges and the opportunities, and in exploring better ways to meet these challenges and capture the opportunities.

> "To have good results, you need to have a combination of fair play, great process and great leadership. The quality of the outcome is largely a consequence of the quality of these three performance pillars. Conversely, shortcomings in one or more of these three pillars invariably lead to quality issues and underperformance."

We often see leaders who focus excessively on results and don't pay enough attention to designing the right processes and building fair personal relationships. To achieve Fair Process Leadership, Ludo Van der Heyden encourages us to pay close attention to the five characteristics of fair play, which philosophers over more than 2,000 years have identified to be the following:

- **Consistency**, or uniformity of treatment across people and time, and thus absence of bias

- **Clarity**, or transparency

- **Communication**, or the ability to give all a voice which they can exercise freely without fear of retribution and retaliation for what is being said

- **Changeability**, or the ability to change course as a function of new information and new facts, which characterizes people that are open to others

- **Culture**, or the commitment to aim to "do the fair thing" not only superficially, but deeply and fundamentally, even at one's expense

Fair play defines and permeates the "quality of the air" when people exchange and engage: the more fair play, the more people will speak up and engage with each other when framing challenges and exploring solutions. Unfair play, on the contrary, stifles debate and creativity.

While Ludo Van der Heyden promotes the "five Cs" as complementary and mutually reinforcing characteristics of fair play, others describe similar aspects as prerequisites to build trust and psychological safety in teams. For us, the five Cs represent our core believes, and our clients tells us that they recognize them in our approach. Together with the client we can change their business for the better by helping them pay more attention to the process and the people involved. Some of the Cs are more difficult to implement than others, but improving communications is usually a quick win. We notice that leaders tend to under-communicate, because they assume that people already know, or they think that their decisions are so obvious that no explanation is needed. Other common pitfalls are to only speak about the "what" and not about the "why" and "how," or to talk about facts and not speak about emotions, or to share a lot of information but not provide the key insights. Finally, there is the risk of engaging too much with the same people and not giving a voice to people who are often not heard in the boardroom. As one of our clients told us:

> "When you asked me how often I met with our young talents, I felt a bit ashamed. Of course I realize this is important, but I don't make enough time for it. You inspired me to start a weekly 'coffee with the CEO' tradition that anyone could sign up for. I also asked my HR Director to invite talents who were less likely to step forward, and those young people especially were able to challenge my assumptions and provide new insights."

We will discuss more on the importance of connecting to people in our next chapter, ENGAGE.

Summary

In this chapter, we covered how you can create the innovation culture that will enable you to build a roadmap for change in your business. We've explored why the traditional project management method is not effective when designing the future of your business in contrast to our approach of Engage, Envision and Explore, which, when creativity is applied correctly in all phases, will bring about successful transformation.

Reflection

Having read through this fifth principle, take a moment to consider the following questions:

- What are the pros and cons of the project management methods you've used in the past?

- How did you apply creative intelligence in the different project phases?

- Are you ready to try a new approach?

PART THREE

THE PRACTICE

6

ENGAGE
Involve And Empower People

"In order for connection to happen, we have to allow ourselves to be seen, really seen."

Brené Brown[1]

Effectiveness = Quality × Acceptance

In this chapter, we explore the importance of connection and involvement of internal and external stakeholders to improve buy-in and quality of your future strategy. We will consider how to ensure each person is allocated an appropriate role in the transformation process, and look at how diversity and inclusivity can be applied to ensure your strategy is a success. First, we will explain why a business innovation journey starts by connecting to the people in and outside your company.

People make the difference between an average result and a great one. When Fennemiek first started out working as a strategy consultant, the role of the consultant was often that of the expert. After doing the analysis, the consultant would come up with their advice on where to go next. Interviews would be held with representatives of the client and the client's customers, but the key objective for this was to collect data. Like most strategy consultants at the time, the primary focus of the consultancy Fennemiek joined was on the quality of their strategies. To prepare for the meeting to present the recommendations, the consultant team would ask themselves questions such as: Is the content accurate? Can the data be trusted? Does the final presentation look professional? At one time, they thought they had developed a winning strategy for a client, and the report still ended up in the famous drawer... At the evaluation, a wise senior consultant shared a famous change management formula: "Effectiveness = Quality × Acceptance."[2] He said:

> "You can develop the best strategies in the world, but if the client doesn't implement them, nothing happens. Sometimes it's better to accept a good enough strategy if it motivates all involved to implement it."

It's a tough lesson to learn for professionals like us who care about the quality of their output, but one we take to heart in our consultancy practice. We pay as much attention to the "acceptance" part of the formula as to the "quality" part, and approach strategy development as a change management process. We involve both internal and external stakeholders in our projects, which improves both the buy-in and the quality of the strategy. We don't provide them with our answers to their challenges, but co-design solutions with them, providing tools, fresh perspectives and the opportunity for them to use their creative intelligence. We've experienced that to ensure progress you need acceptance and, better yet, ownership of the key stakeholders involved. The objective is to empower the team that will be responsible for implementation and make sure they feel that the new strategic direction is their own idea. And of course, we also bring in people with relevant experience and expertise from inside and outside the company to jointly come up with the best ideas.

To be able to design the right role in the process for all involved, you need to start with mapping the different stakeholders and understanding their potential impact on the project. People who have a great interest in the project, and a high influence on the result, all need to take part in the business innovation journey. Depending on their needs, mindset and personal skills, specific roles need to be designed for them in the project. For example, you can ask them to participate as a "devil's advocate" to challenge your assumptions, act as a critical customer to stress-test your first concepts, be on a selection panel when the teams pitch their new business ideas or show up as a mystery guest acting as a customer. Investing more time to get the key stakeholders on board in the development phase saves time during the implementation phase later. While this is common practice in change management, it is not always in business innovation.

Keep in mind that business innovation requires transformation and apply other success factors from change management as well. Examples are focusing on the guiding coalition of the willing as we described in Chapter 3: CARE, identifying and involving change ambassadors (the entrepreneurial style managers we wrote about in Chapter 4: LEARN) from the start and communicating quick wins.

WHICH ROLE SHOULD THE DIFFERENT STAKEHOLDERS HAVE IN THE PROCESS?

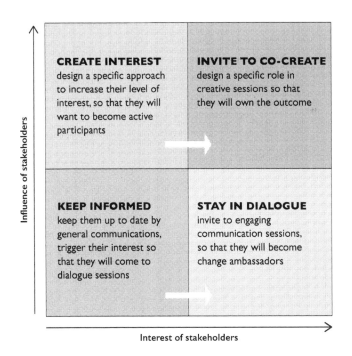

This model is based on the stakeholder matrix of Mendelow.[3] We use it to map stakeholders and discuss which roles we should design for them in the business innovation process.

Understanding pains and gains

Henry Ford famously said, "If I would have asked my customers what they wanted, they would have said faster horses."[4] If you want to improve your current business, you can ask your customers for feedback, but when it's time to design a new business, you should ask them a different type of question. What would the ideal situation look like from their point of view? What is it that they want to accomplish? What would make them happy while doing so? What kind of hurdles and irritations do they experience? These customer needs are also known as the "pains and gains," courtesy of Alexander Osterwalder's useful value proposition canvas.[5] A research agency can collect customer insights and present the results, which can be a good start. However, we feel that in an innovation journey, it's important for the participants to experience the customer needs themselves. This can be done by going on a consumer safari together, as food and beverage companies often do, or by conducting street interviews. Projective techniques can also work well in this phase, encouraging people to walk in somebody else's shoes and play-act the role of their customer. Alternatively, you can ask customers to be involved in the ENVISION phase, co-creating the future with them, but we agree with Henry Ford that this works better for incremental innovation.

For a consumer company targeting teenage girls, we invited the participants of an innovation lab to ask for the help of a daughter, niece or another young girl they knew. The girls were given a little sketchbook and asked to draw or select pictures of 20 of their favorite objects. The innovation lab participants were asked to describe the girl as a fictional character, a so-called persona, using a different name. In the session, the first exercise was to deep dive into the worlds of those teenage girls, trying to match their sketchbooks to the right persona. The objective is not only to collect insights into their preferences but to put participants in the right frame of mind for the creative session through a shared experience.

Sometimes this shared experience to start a creative session can stretch people's comfort zone. We have partnered a few times with Peter Rombouts, who is both a professional tango dancer and an organizational expert.[6] We invite him in when our clients deal with a wicked problem that they have discussed intensively, and we see that talking about it more won't help. They need new insights to get unstuck. For example, one of our clients was dealing with a complex ecosystem of business-to-business partnerships and wanted to better understand why there was so little flow. She met with the individual partners, but they weren't able – or willing – to tell her what was wrong. When she asked Peter the same question, he was able to show her through his dance what was going on. As he explained it:

> "I always start from a question. We speak about it for a
> short while and then I ask permission to dance it. When
> I stand up, I listen and feel deeply and let my body move.
> This allows me to explore and expose a deeper layer. It
> makes the essence of what needs to be looked at visible
> for all that watch me."

While he was dancing, and by doing so showing specific movements and patterns around the question, the other participants of the session were sitting in a circle around him. If you were too uncomfortable with this, you were allowed to leave. Almost everyone stayed, although some were skeptical. After a first round, when everybody had a chance to reflect on what they saw and felt, he invited people to join him. They were asked to dance the role of the partners in the ecosystem. It was telling that some of the most skeptical people stood up to dance. As our client said:

> "It's hard to explain what cannot be explained rationally.
> You need to experience it to feel the power of this dance
> dialogue. It's now almost a year ago that we organized
> this session, and, looking back, it was a tipping point. By
> watching Peter dance, I felt what I needed to change in
> the relationship to create impact."

The target audience can also be an internal one. A biobased technology company asked us to help develop the future direction of the internal R&D department. We encouraged the team to better understand the needs of their new boss, the Chief Technology Officer (CTO), by giving them "pains and gains" questions to prepare for the session. What did they think the new CTO would want to accomplish in the board? Based on their insights, they developed an onboarding present, learning even more from the conversation they had with him when they presented it. This assignment allowed for valuable input to design the future R&D department, while also being an effective team development exercise. Whenever possible, we design our creative sessions to realize both business development and organizational learning objectives.

WHAT QUESTIONS SHOULD YOU ASK TO UNDERSTAND YOUR CUSTOMERS' NEEDS?

	PAINS What are your biggest frustrations?	**GAINS** What makes you really happy?
EXPERIENCE with the business/ product/service		
TODAY 24 hours in your life		
FUTURE aspirations and dreams		

We create specific questions related to the future challenge and the individual audience to uncover their relevant pains and gains, starting from the different perspectives that are illustrated above.

Include outsiders in your team

Innovation requires looking at the world from different perspectives and developing new connections between existing ideas, which is a key characteristic of creative people as we explained in Chapter 4: LEARN. The need for multiple perspectives is one of the reasons you need interdisciplinary teams for innovation. But corporate reality is often different. In the years that we've worked as innovation partners across various industries and countries, we have seen a lot of silos. Most "birds of one feather tend to stick together" and allow little room for people who think differently. Without even realizing it, organizations and departments have developed their own sets of unspoken rules – behavioral constraints that are not talked about or written down. Social psychologist Irving Janis from Yale University introduced the term groupthink to describe how members of a group can be so focused on striving for unanimity that it overrides their motivation to explore alternative courses of action:

> "Groupthink refers to a deterioration of mental efficiency, reality testing, and moral judgment that results from in-group pressures. These groups are over-cohesive. Because of a need to belong to the group, no one wants to break the peace and express a contrary view."[7]

Examples of groupthink fiascos studied by Janis include the United States' failure to anticipate the attack on Pearl Harbor, the Bay of Pigs invasion, the escalation of Vietnam war and the ill-fated hostage rescue in Iran. Groupthink is a threat for creativity because it leads to self-censorship. People don't bring up alternatives, or potential risks, for fear of upsetting the status quo. Groupthink is common, and all organizations are vulnerable to it, especially when the people working for it are similar in backgrounds and the leader is strong.

Like the overconfidence bias we referred to in Chapter 4: LEARN, groupthink is another human bias that we need to acknowledge and counterbalance in innovation projects. Fortunately, we've experienced that it is relatively easy to break existing patterns in a specific project, while it's much more challenging to change patterns structurally in an organization. Bringing in unusual outsiders that are willing to challenge the status quo will encourage the whole team to use their explorative mindset and result in more innovative ideas. For example, the famous pointed front shape of the Japanese bullet train was inspired by the beak of the kingfisher.[8] This aerodynamic shape was the answer to a sound problem the engineers encountered and ended up saving them 10% to 15% in energy usage as well. This creative solution was made possible because one of the engineers on the design team was an avid bird watcher in his free time.

One outsider can easily be overruled. In our business innovation projects, we have experienced that you need to bring in at least three outsiders to counterbalance groupthink. Some companies take this a step further and create a group that consists only of outsiders to challenge their thinking. Microsoft in the Netherlands has introduced the concept of "the Council of Difference." Gonnie Been, at the time responsible for social innovation at Microsoft, told us:

> "For some questions such as 'how to improve diversity' you need the eyes of outsiders. We created the concept of the Council of Difference to provide us with unusual perspectives and stimulate a different type of dialogue. We invite different groups, like 16 to 20-year-olds or people with a disability, and give them free access to the company for three months. Afterwards, they share their observations with the board, which result both in meaningful conversations and concrete actions."

Diversity makes teams better

Most companies now actively focus on increasing diversity and inclusion, although sometimes we feel the interpretation of diversity is somewhat narrow. The focus tends to be on gender, ethnicity and age, while we would like to look at diversity in terms of the different mindsets and leadership styles that we wrote about in Chapter 4: LEARN.

Luckily, more and more business leaders interpret diversity in this broader sense. Accenture research among 200 human resources executives from global companies concluded that many leaders are realizing that they need people who significantly differ from each other in the top of their businesses.[9] A HR leader they surveyed said:

> "Top leadership groups in the future will be characterized by people with great diversity of experience and thought styles — for example, are they more analytical or more 'by the gut?' These forms of diversity will be even more important than diversity of age, nationality and gender."

When we spoke about diversity in the interviews we did for this book, we got mixed reactions. Some were tired of the diversity discussion and stressed that you should pick the best person for the job. Most, however, recognized the value of diversity especially for decision-making. A hopeful perspective since companies will not only improve their decision-making by creating more diverse leadership teams, but also their innovation capabilities and their ability to embrace change. As the CEO of an international company said:

> "Even though we were active globally, our leadership team for a long time wasn't. Now that different nationalities have joined the board, we are looking at problems from more different angles. It's true that it has become more difficult to automatically understand each other, but I also think we make better decisions because of this."

How can you make sure that diverse perspectives lead to applied creativity and not to endless discussions? How can leaders deal with increasing differences in their team and still steer the project in one direction? Leaders will need to lead collectively as a team. Accenture proposes the name "ensemble leadership" for this, comparing it to how a musical ensemble is organized – a metaphor that speaks to us because it's easy to picture. A successful ensemble can perform equally well in the intimacy of a quartet, the relative formality of a chamber group or the tight structure of a symphony orchestra. An ensemble leader may be called upon to be strong and visible, as in the case of a symphony. At other times, for example in a chamber orchestra, the conductor will lead while playing amid the group, or the group may perform entirely without a conductor. In all these examples the leader empowers his team to perform. Shared under-standing — forged through the common experience of tackling difficult scores — and a desire to improve through practice give musical ensembles the agility to operate under widely varying condi-tions. As we explained in Chapter 3: CARE, shared purpose and values are the foundation for this type of agility.

We also like the ensemble analogy because it shows that the kind of musical instruments you need depends on the music you want to play. In other words, each business innovation challenge requires a tailor-made diverse team to address it. Designing the project team that will create the future of your business is as important as designing the process and the potential solutions. We recommend combining insiders with outsiders, big-picture perspectives with niche expertise and unusual thinkers with creative makers in your design team. It doesn't end there. You also need to create the right type of trusted environment for this diversity to work. As Brené Brown so beautifully put it in her TED Talk about the power of vulnerability, real connec-tion (and creativity, we would add) only happens when people allow themselves to be really seen.

Summary

In this chapter, we reflected on the importance of starting with designing the project team, involving key stakeholders and understanding the needs of your target audiences when designing the future of your business. Including people from inside and outside the business in the creation of your strategy improves the quality of the strategy developed and ensures the buy-in of stakeholders internally and externally.

We've also covered how a diverse group of stakeholders can contribute to an effective development and implementation of a new future direction. Key to the success of that is to allocate the right roles to each person so that they can utilize their skills and experience to help realize a successful business transformation.

Reflection

Having read through this sixth principle, take a moment to consider the following questions:

- How have you engaged people in your business strategy projects?
- Is groupthink an issue in your organization?
- Are there any outsiders who had an impact on you and your team?

7

ENVISION
Imagine A Better Future

"The future belongs to those who
believe in the power of their dreams."

Eleanor Roosevelt[i]

Starting from the future

We see business innovation as a design challenge: what do you want your business to look like in the future? In the same way that a designer partners with a client to create new products, we help you create a shared vision of the desired future for your business. This vision needs to be both aspirational and realistic – a dream that people can believe in so that it becomes theirs as Eleanor Roosevelt's quote expresses.

To create that vision of your future business, we will give you a model to identify the key drivers for change in your industry and discuss the methods we use to help design the future direction of your business. As we showed in Chapter 3: CARE, you can start from today's situation if your goal is to optimize, but transformation requires starting from the future. Your purpose and values serve as the touchstone to understand which way to grow. Depending on your strategic challenge, the future can be a few years from now or much further away. Once you have created your future direction, you will understand how you can position yourself tomorrow and take the first step to where you want to be.

WHAT DO YOU WANT YOUR BUSINESS TO LOOK LIKE IN THE FUTURE?

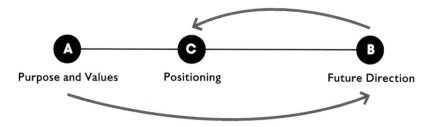

Your purpose and values are your guide when creating future directions. Once you have decided where you want to go, you will see how you can position yourself tomorrow as a first step in getting there.

Traditionally, strategy development starts with an analysis of the market, competitive position and customer needs. Now we begin the process with creating the desired end state. That doesn't mean analysis is not important, but the process starts the other way around. This is the future-led approach that characterizes a design process, and which is well described in **Lead from the Future: How to turn visionary thinking into breakthrough growth**.[2] Future-back thinking and planning begins with sensing and envisioning, and actively and imaginatively immersing yourself in your future environment to define your desired destination. This approach invites you to set aside your assumptions about the way things work today and think outside the box by using your creative intelligence.

To design new future directions, you need to risk giving up your comfort zone, embrace the unknown, dare to break conventions and allow yourself to make mistakes as we described in Chapter 4: LEARN. This requires creative courage. As the French author André Gide beautifully writes, "You cannot discover new oceans unless you have the courage to lose sight of the shore."[3]

In our business innovation journeys, we challenge the leadership teams we work with to create a big, bold dream of what the company could be capable of, to shape both a better business and a better world. Patagonia is a company that is known for using business to inspire and implement solutions to the environmental crisis. Founder Yvon Chouinard writes about how he developed this vision in his book *Let my People Go Surfing: The education of a reluctant businessman*:

> "I took a dozen of my top managers to Argentina, to the windswept mountains of the real Patagonia, for a walk-about. In the course of roaming around those wildlands, we asked ourselves why we were in business and what kind of business we wanted Patagonia to be."[4]

Patagonia is a well-known example of an activist brand and a pioneer in sustainability. It's also an example of a company that was purpose-driven from the start, embodying the values of founder Yvon Chouinard. Other companies transform into a purpose-driven businesses in following lifecycles. Lego started as a brick manufacturer and developed the vision to be a global force for learning through play.[5] Beyond selling toys, they are committed to creating a better, brighter world for children to inherit, reaching millions of kids annually through their community engagement programs. The challenge is to translate your ambition of creating a better future into a clear image of what your business could look like. Sebastiaan van Dam, one of the founders of the scale-up Being Development, expressed it as follows:

> "The reputation of real estate developers is that they are only in the business to make money. We are a new generation of developers and have the ambition to do things differently, but how? The creative sessions helped us to imagine our desired future. Ideally, the environments we build empower communities and make the world a happier and healthier place."

What would you like the future of your business to look like?

Creating scenarios for a changing world

We invite you to open your eyes to your environment and identify the key drivers of change in your industry. What are the relevant trends and opportunities? What could your world look like 20 years from now? One of the ways to do this is through scenario-planning, an approach that originated in public policy and was brought to the business world by Shell in the early 1970s.[6] The model invites you to select the two main drivers of change in your world and put them on the X and Y axes. Shell at that time had oil prices (sharp rise versus decrease) on one axis and oil exporting countries (friendly versus hostile) on the other. For each of the four quadrants you ask yourself the "what if?" question: what would our world look like if this happens? As Shell puts it:

> "Shell scenarios encourage leaders to consider events that may only be remote possibilities and stretch their thinking. Our scenarios help people understand possibilities and uncertainties ahead."[7]

Collecting relevant trend reports and making a trend analysis is a good start. We often use the PESTLE model in sessions because it inspires people to look beyond the trends in their own industry.[8] PESTLE is an acronym for:

- **Political**: what are the geo-political trends, such as the war in the Ukraine, that may affect your business?

- **Economic**: which factors will impact your economic performance, such as the current high level of inflation?

- **Social**: what are relevant demographic and social trends, such as the growing social gap?

- **Technological**: which of the technologies of the Fourth Industrial Revolution will disrupt your business?

- **Legal**: which laws that might influence your business do you expect to change?

- **Environmental**: which ecological factors, such as the rise in temperature, will directly influence you?

Once you have a longlist of potentially relevant trends, you need to decide which are the key ones you will use as the foundation for creating your future scenarios. To stimulate ownership and alignment, we ask the team to do this together using the tool in the illustration and validating their choices with futurists and industry experts.

WHICH ARE THE KEY TRENDS THAT WILL IMPACT YOUR FUTURE?

INDUSTRY IMPACT	–	–	– / +
BUSINESS IMPACT	–	+	+ / +
	OLD NEWS	**TODAY**	**FUTURE**

We use this tool to facilitate the dialogue on which trends to use as the foundation for your future scenarios. For example, imagine you are discussing the "wearable technology" trend in fashion. You might conclude that it has a low impact in the industry today and will become more important in the future. For your business, however, you feel it will have a high impact in the future and a medium impact today. Another trend, such as personification, could already be "old news."

The first step is the rational understanding of where your world may be heading. Next, we invite the team to immerse themselves in the future so they can let go of today's boundaries and design their business as if they are starting from scratch. Creative people – who tend to think in images – do this intuitively, but others need help to really feel it. This is where creative storytellers can make a difference. For an engineering company, for example, we asked a science fiction writer to help. They turned the four future scenarios they had developed based on their two key drivers of change (geopolitics: harmony versus conflict; energy transition: slow versus fast) into engaging stories. To invite the team to step into the four different worlds, their stories were very expressive and addressed the reader personally ("It's 2030, you are…"), immediately evoking images of what those futures looked like in the readers' minds.

It's not always necessary to use different scenarios. You can also develop a single shared vision on what the future will be like and bring only that scenario to life. We like to engage the support of artists for this part of the journey. For example, for an education publisher, we partnered with theater makers. They created a play that helped the participants of the creative sessions to understand the changing expectations of future students. As the publisher said afterwards:

> "We had often talked about blended learning and how students are able to get their education from world leading institutions online, but we approached it very rationally. We didn't really feel the sense of urgency because our business was still doing OK. Watching the play, seeing how these trends would change their lives and disrupt our industry, changed that."

Designing future directions for your business

We call the different options for the desired future state of your business "future directions" to distinguish them from "future scenarios" – a term that is commonly used to describe potential futures for the outside environment. The difference is that future scenarios visualize what you think your part of the world may look like an x number of years from now, while you describe in your possible future directions what your business could be within this world. Once your imagination has transported you to the future scenario, you can visualize your own desired role in this. We stimulate this by using creative tools that encourage you to go beyond your cognitive intelligence and tap into your other senses. Some examples of creative exercises that can help to achieve this are inviting you to select images to represent your dream for the company, using business examples from outside your industry as a creative springboard or using the brainstorming tools we described in Chapter 5: ACT.

For the previously mentioned education publishers, we used a storytelling exercise. They had developed a future scenario based on the flipped classroom principle, with students being able to access short movies from top-notch speakers instead of going to a classroom to listen to their professors. In this scenario, the class-room would become a place for reflection and dialogue requiring different learning tools to support this from the publisher. We asked the team to imagine that it was 2030 and they were preparing a TED Talk. What did they want the audience to remember about the added value of their business? Which examples from their daily business would they use to prove this claim?

Another creative method is to use "how might we?" questions as a starting point for ideation. Sid Parnes first introduced this approach in 1967 in his **Creative Behavior Guidebook**.[9] Imagine how Kodak would have used this method to design a new future direction starting from their purpose to share the big moments in your life. Their questions might have included:

- How might we capture the big moments in life?
- How might we convince people to trust us with those moments?
- How might we share big moments without using images?

Similarly, you can start with "what if?" questions, a technique that comes intuitively to creative people. It was first described in 1977 by creative thinking expert Edward de Bono in his book **Lateral Thinking**.[10] "What if?" questions invite you to use your imagination to explore the key elements that influence the future. The right type of question challenges your assumptions, shifts people's think-ing and serves as a catalyst for change.

WHAT IS THE STORY YOU WOULD LIKE TO SHARE ABOUT YOUR BUSINESS?

A FUTURE STORY	
GOAL	Who is your audience?
	What do you want to achieve with this story?
QUESTIONS	Where will we be in five years?
	What must have happened?
	What is the story about?
	What are we proud of?
	What does success look like?
	How do we create value and impact?
STRUCTURE	Describe the take away of your story
	Start strong, make your point, finish even stronger
	Invite, seduce, take audience along: imagine? What if… ?
	Use good examples from your daily business to proof your claim
	Make a bridge to your goal, your dream.
THREE KEY POINTS	What happened?
	What was successful?
	What are we proud of?
END AND CONCLUSION	What is your point?
	How do you want to be remembered?

This tool encourages you to prioritize and select a single and consistent message about your future direction. What is it that you want your audience to remember about your business? Everything else you want to tell them can be used as supporting evidence for your core message.

Duncan Wardle, former Head of Innovation and Creativity at Disney Parks, explains how Walt Disney's concept of Disneyland started with his ambition for his movie *Fantasia* in 1955.[11] Walt Disney wanted to create a new way to immerse his audience in his stories. What if he could control the environment? As we know now, this resulted in a new business direction rather than a new type of movie theater.

What are the "what if?" questions for your business? These kinds of exercises provide inspiration for the creation of future directions for your business. To design possible future directions that go beyond the obvious, you need creative intelligence and a team with different perspectives, expertise and skills. This diverse team should be handpicked for the challenge as explained in Chapter 6: ENGAGE. Besides inviting people from your own company, you also need people from the outside. In the ENGAGE phase, you develop the ideal profile of the team and the outsiders you would like to engage for your specific question.

In the case of the engineering company, where energy transition was a key topic, we naturally invited different types of experts from this field. The outsiders included a technology professor, a regulation expert, an energy transition consultant and a business leader from another industry that was a few steps ahead of our client in this transition. Finding the right type of expert is not always that obvious. For the consumer company targeting teenage girls that we referred to in ENGAGE, a key topic for their future direction was the need to innovate on how to handle their products. We wanted experts on quick finger work and dexterity, which first led us to think of inviting a pickpocket, but eventually we found a leading designer of tricks for magicians who challenged the whole team to think in different ways. As the company's Innovation Director said:

> "It was the co-creation with our people and the designer of the magicians' tricks that made the difference. We've never ended up with so many different new ideas from one workshop before. Our technical experts understand what's possible and are very creative when it comes to developing new materials and applications, the co-creation triggered them to go a step further and come up with new strategic directions."

The bigger the transformation you need to make, the more outsiders you need to contribute fresh perspectives. We see creating the future of your business as a design challenge and recommend to co-create possible futures in small design teams in well-structured creative sessions. We advise our clients to organize these sessions as a pressure cooker at a location outside of the office, where the team stays in the bubble, and you can keep up the momentum.

The power of positivity

Once you have developed your future direction, how do you describe it? This may seem like a minor detail, but helping people to "see the light" is the first step in realizing business transformation as we explained in Chapter 3: CARE.

In **CEO Excellence**, three McKinsey partners describe the six mindsets that distinguish the best leaders from the rest, based on their research among their selection of top 200 CEOs.[12] The first mindset is about direction-setting and daring to be bold. The CEOs they interviewed talked about the importance of reframing the game for internal motivation. For example, from the start Netflix founder Reed Hastings never expressed the ambition to be the number one DVD company. Instead, he talked about his dream to become "a global entertainment distribution company that provides a unique channel for film producers and studios." The way you talk about your future direction matters.

As early as the ENVISION phase, we ask the teams to come up with a short statement that expresses each of their possible future directions in an inspiring way. We use these also as working titles to be able to discuss and explore the consequences of each direction in the next EXPLORE phase. We recommend them to focus on "seeing the light," because talking about the future as an opportunity inspires people in a more sustainable way than communicating risks ever can. This becomes very clear when we look at major problems such as the COVID pandemic or climate change. While the lockdown caused people to work at home in the first place, it's the longing for a better work-life balance that inspires people to continue to do so. Linda Steg, Professor of Environmental Psychology at the University of Groningen, and her PhD student Anne van Valkengoed showed that negative framing of climate change can lead to anxiety, denial and complacency.[13] When the message was framed as an opportunity and people were led to believe they could make a positive contribution, behavioral change happened more often.

To paraphrase Antoine de Saint-Exupéry, the French pioneering aviator and writer of **Le Petit Prince**, "If you want people to build a boat, you first have to make them long for the sea." [14] You will only make people "long for the sea" and inspire them to act when your story about the future combines the rational and the emotional, touching people's minds and hearts. Storytelling is a key creative leadership skill in transformation journeys.

Counterintuitively, to be able to focus on the positive, you first need to address the negative. Problems and fears that remain unmentioned can become even bigger and dominate the discussion even when nobody speaks about them. We often include the "elephants in the room" exercise to first clear the air. We invite people to list the important topics and controversial issues that they think are obvious to everyone involved, but normally don't get mentioned because they cause embarrassment or people have already given up on solving them. As we explained in Chapter 5: ACT, open communication builds trust and creates an environment that allows for creativity. Understanding the elephants in the room is a necessary step in shifting to a positive mindset and is also part of developing a roadmap, as we'll look at in the next chapter.

Summary

In this chapter, we covered the importance of visualizing what you want your business to look like in the future. We've identified the methods we use to design the future direction of your business once you have established the key drivers for change in your industry.

Essential to bringing the future direction of your business to life is the power of positivity and the understanding that how you talk about your business matters. A constructive dialogue about the future can only be facilitated when you embrace the right mindset to create trust and allow for creativity.

Reflection

Having read through this seventh principle, take a moment to consider the following questions:

- Could you imagine a better future for your business?
- Are you prepared to let go of the status quo?
- What kind of narrative do you use when explaining your strategy?

EXPLORE
Make It Happen

"It always seems impossible until it's done."

Nelson Mandela[1]

The charm of three

In this chapter, we will investigate how to identify the key shifts needed to implement your business transformation and how to design a roadmap that will help you arrive at your desired destination. Finally, we'll demonstrate the importance of continuous exploration and will look at how you can do this as you pursue your business innovation journey. But first, let's begin by exploring the need to have three strategic options for decision-making.

Once you have designed your possible future directions in the ENVISION phase, the next phase starts: EXPLORE. In this phase, you decide which of the potential directions to choose and develop the roadmap of how to get there. This can be done with the same core team as in the ENVISION phase, without the outsiders. Instead, we recommend adding functional experts (such as IT, HR, Finance) and other key stakeholders that have been identified in the ENGAGE phase. Together they explore which business and leadership trans-formations are needed to make the desired futures a reality.

We've learned over the years that presenting three options for decision-making works best. One choice isn't a choice, and having two makes it a black and white conversation. People will immediately decide one option is right, and the other is wrong. When you give people three options, they will consider all three and take time to think through the options. To create clarity about the efforts that are needed to realize each direction, we encourage people to make them as bold and outspoken as possible. Keep in mind Nelson Mandela's encouraging words, and don't be afraid to aim for what today feels impossible. There will always be the opportunity later to start with smaller steps and to combine elements of all three potential options in the final direction.

Being, the real estate developer we wrote about in Chapter 7: ENVISION for example, expressed the ambition to be a different type of developer, creating positive impact. Together, we explored three different future directions. "Leading the real estate revolution" focused on their role, leading by example and creating a movement to change the whole industry. "The sustainable frontrunner" acknowledged their pioneer position and would oblige them to keep on innovating to stay ahead of the game. Lastly, the essence of "creating better places for humanity" was to develop happier and healthier environments for people. After we mapped the consequences of each direction, they decided to go for the third option, integrating some of the elements of the other two options. As Sebastiaan van Dam and Dirk Dekker, the founders of Being, said afterwards:

> "All three of the future directions represented our vision, which to us was totally clear, but after the creative sessions we understood why it confused people. Choosing one overarching concept, using some of the other elements as supporting evidence, provided the necessary clarity. Being able to give both our own team and our partners a clear image of where we want to go motivates them and gives direction to everything we do."

For a next economy campus that aimed to be a catalyst for developing a regional innovation ecosystem, we also explored the potential of three future directions. "Playground for digital innovators" was chosen, reflecting the vision to be a virtual place to experiment together. When we identified the consequences of each direction in our work sessions, they concluded that this one fitted their people the best, was the most attractive to their future audiences and they trusted they could make it happen.

What is your "impossible" ambition? Can you split it up in three potential directions?

Identifying the key shifts

Before you decide on a future direction, we encourage you to visualize the desired end state for the specific elements of your organization, including:

- the business model and types of revenues
- products and services
- brand strategy and design
- sales and marketing
- culture and leadership

If you compare this with where you are today, what would you say are the key shifts needed to realize the transformation? It helps to use a simple "from… to…" format and limit yourself to a maximum of ten key shifts. When we partnered with a family business in ceramics, for example, the key shifts the team identified included:

- "From a focus on the consumer market to a business-to-business focus."
- "From product development and sales to co-development and manufacturing."
- "From own distribution to partnerships."

HOW DO YOU GET FROM A TO B?

KEY SHIFTS

Business model and types of revenue

From .... to ....

From .... to ....

Products and services

From .... to ....

From .... to ....

Brand strategy and design

From .... to ....

From .... to ....

Sales and marketing

From .... to ....

From .... to ....

Culture and leadership

From .... to ....

From .... to ....

This tool helps you to facilitate the dialogue which are the key shifts you need to realize. A business transformation program includes roadmaps for each of those key shifts.

To help uncover the key shifts, we use creative exercises such as doing a premortem. This is a prospective hindsight tool developed by Nobel Prize winner Daniel Kahneman and Gary Klein.[2] It stimulates the implicit knowledge in the group by asking them to imagine it's ten years after they have introduced their new business direction. One team gets the assignment to pretend that it was a big success, the

other that it was a great disaster. The next step is to write down –
first individually and later as a group – the reasons for this success
or failure. The challenge is to be as specific as possible, and to be
courageous enough to ignore the hidden rules, company politics and
other elephants in the room. In an open dialogue, you can uncover
the key success criteria, and, from there, the shifts that are needed.
It sounds simple, but the beauty of it is that Kahneman collected
compelling evidence that this approach generates better plans and
decisions. The reason for this is that "the imaginary situation" helps
to deal with human biases such as being overly optimistic and striving
for consensus that we wrote about in LEARN and ENGAGE.

Focusing on imaginary situations also helps you to get unstuck when
you don't agree on a direction. One of our clients, a car paint company,
identified smart cars as a game-changer for their business. After all,
their turnover came mostly from auto repair shops, repainting cars
after accidents. Smart cars mean less accidents, which is good news
for the world but was a threat for this company's revenues. The big
question was how much time they had to design a second curve for
their business, a concept we explained in Chapter 1: CREATE.

Half of the team believed their process was a slow evolutionary one
and they still had time (A), while the other half was convinced that
it would disrupt their market and they had to act now (B). Instead
of trying to get them to agree, we split them up and turned it into
a debate. We purposefully designed each team to include believers
from both sides, asking them to imagine they were in favor of A or B
and defend this direction wholeheartedly. We then invited them to
play-act specific roles when the other team was presenting and ask
questions from that perspective (such as an auto repair shop owner,
a R&D person and a trade association representative). We laughed
a lot during the creative session, but as the Business Development
Director from the team said:

"We had fun together, but the session also resulted in a sound list of trends we could use to track the speed of change. And most importantly, we agreed that no matter how fast our world would change, we would still need to design our new future direction now."

Dream big, start small

The roadmap for how to get from A to B includes different tracks for the big shifts needed. For each track, you define a plan as usual, for example using the OGSM tool.[3] We like this method, because it encourages you to summarize your Objectives, Goals, Strategies and Measures on one page. Keep in mind that the objectives need to stay aspirational and describe the desired end state for each track in such a way that people can imagine it and want to go end up there. This is where creative storytelling skills are needed. As CEO Rudy Stroink, CEO at furniture company Pastoe told us:

> "Making sure that people can see the dream for themselves is key. Since I'm trained as an architect, I often start with sketches. Soon after, those are translated into an enticing story illustrated with images. I grew up in the United States, and there I learned the value of storytelling. This is something CEOs should be trained to do more often. With the right story, you can truly engage your audiences and create enthusiasm for your ideas. Storytelling is a force that makes things move."

Another difference is in how you execute the plan. As we explained in Chapter 5: ACT, business innovation is not a linear process but an iterative one. Your roadmap serves as a guide for the general direction, but along the way you learn by experimenting, succeeding, failing and adjusting. Even when your experiments fail from a business point of view, they will still be a success from a learning point of view. In this part of the EXPLORE phase, we help you set up experiments to stress-test your ideas and generate insights on how to scale the business opportunity. Sometimes we do this for all three directions to help you decide which one has the most potential; in other cases, we focus on the chosen direction.

Experiments can be small or quite sizable in terms of the investments needed in resources, budget and time. The smaller ones are designed to fail quickly and cheaply, just like the prototypes of designers. The more sizable ones are comparable to a start-up and come with a higher risk. The impact of the potential failure has been identified upfront. To give you a few examples:

- A quick and dirty way to test a concept is to make a conceptual prototype and show it to people inside and outside your company to collect feedback. We used this for an innovation lab concept, creating a mock-up of what this could look like.

- The real estate developers adjusted their sales presentation as if they had already gone to the desired transformation and invited some trusted partners to a "fake" pitch, which is another quick way to stress-test.

- For the education publisher, we organized two different events for schoolteachers, each one reflecting the style and desired experience of a different direction, to understand how attractive the new proposition was for their audience, and how motivating it was for their team.

- The health tech company found a partner to co-develop a pilot project, creating a dedicated team to set it up as a separate business. As much as testing the new strategic direction, it tested their ambition of developing an innovation ecosystem.

Once you've done some smaller experiments and feel confident you've chosen the right direction, the key question becomes whether you can do this in your existing organization or if you need to set up a new company. The bigger the gap between the current and desired direction and culture, the bigger the necessity to separate this team from the rest. An internal start-up needs autonomy and the freedom to deviate from the usual corporate rules. This requires sponsorship and protection from the board.

Exploration is an ongoing journey

EXPLORE is the last phase of the project to design your future direction, and at the same time a continuous state of mind. As we described in Chapter 1: CREATE, accelerated change means that businesses need to be agile and adjust their direction more often than before. In their book *Never Done*, philosopher Martijn Aslander and journalist Erwin Witteveen frame this as being in a state of "permanent beta."[4] Beta is a software term that is used to indicate the version of a product that isn't completely ready but is almost there. They argue that once we acknowledge that we're in a state of perpetual beta because there just isn't enough time to develop perfect permanent solutions, big improvements in business, healthcare and education are possible. They invite us to look at all solutions as temporarily and to keep on improving ourselves. Do you recognize the value of this approach in your business?

We agree with them that innovation requires continuous adaption and learning. This starts with self-reflection: the ability to critically look at your own thoughts, emotions, actions and decisions with the aim to learn from them. If you're satisfied with everything you do, there is no room for improvement. Instead of evaluating a project when it's over, find regular moments during the process to evaluate. For creative people, this is a fun journey. As explorer Don Walsh said, "Exploration is curiosity put into action."[5]

When we are invited to talk about this principle in leadership development programs, we often get the reaction, "This sounds exasperating, how do you ever know it's good enough? How can you plan this type of process?" This is a typical left-brain reaction as we showed in Chapter 4: LEARN, but this reaction also makes sense. For the whole company to be in constant motion is too much, so you need to find the right balance between organizational stability and agility.

As we wrote in Chapter 6: ENGAGE, we often learn from change management processes. John Kotter, a leading expert in this field, provides practical inspiration on how to do this in his book *Accelerate: Building strategic agility for a faster-moving world*.[6] His advice is to embrace the both/and approach that we spoke about as ambidexterity in LEARN. He describes how one part of the organization should focus on what you know and currently do well, and the other on where you want to go in the future. In CREATE, we referred to this as "exploit what is" versus "create what is not yet." The part that is focused on the current business works well with hierarchy, linear processes and control, while the future-oriented part requires a network organization, iterative processes and embracing uncertainty. Our work, and this book, focuses on developing the "create what is not yet" part of business that benefits from the network organization Kotter describes. Most companies we work with include a key organizational structure shift from hierarchy only towards also developing innovation ecosystems (with internal and external networks) in their "from-to" ambition list.

Another major shift our clients want to realize is in culture and leadership. The perpetual beta state we live in requires an explorative mind and creativity as we've demonstrated throughout this book, but which creative skills do you need to develop in practice? To determine this for your specific strategic challenge and team, one of the tools we use is based on *Metaskills* by Marty Neumeier.[7] He argues that technology will replace every job that doesn't need a high degree of creativity, humanity or leadership, and encourages people to develop five "metaskills." We make use of his five skills but have adjusted the descriptions somewhat to link them to the business innovation journey. They are:

- **Feeling**: empathy and intuition
- **Seeing**: bigger picture and opportunity spotting
- **Dreaming**: envisioning and ideation
- **Making**: experimenting and prototyping
- **Learning**: intrinsic motivation and self-reflection

When the R&D team of the biobased technology company we mentioned earlier mapped their current and desired metaskills, they discovered that within each metaskill they had both strengths and weaknesses. For example, within "making," they were good at finding partners but needed to develop their accepting failure skill. Looking back at the session, the Innovation Director said:

> "The workshop gave us a new perspective on what the 'ideal' innovation leader looks like, and what skills we need both as a team and individually. In the follow up sessions, we created personal development plans for each of us, including assignments like doing an activity that stretches your comfort zone every week, contributing to our company's festival of personal failures, and participating in an improvisation lab to practice storytelling."

WHAT METASKILLS DO YOU NEED TO DEVELOP TO KEEP ON EXPLORING?

METASKILLS
FEELING EMPATHY AND INTUITION What skills do we need to truly understand the needs of others?
SEEING BIGGER PICTURE AND OPPORTUNITY SPOTTING What skills do we need to open our eyes for possible futures?
DREAMING ENVISIONING AND IDEATION What skills do we need to imagine possible futures and create new ideas?
MAKING EXPERIMENTING AND PROTOTYPING What skills do we need for concept development and creating models?
LEARNING INTRINSIC MOTIVATION AND SELF-REFLECTION What are the main skills to continuously improve ourselves?

This tool is based on the metaskills concept by Marty Neumeier. We use it to facilitate the dialogue about which creative skills you want to develop on a team and personal level to embrace EXPLORE as a permanent state of being.

Summary

In this chapter, we covered the benefit of having three future direction options for decision-making. We looked at visualizing the end state for all functional aspects of your business to identify the key shifts your organization will need to make to implement the desired transformation. We explored the importance of ongoing exploration once the transformation has been implemented to acknowledge the fact that the need to improve your business is always present and to ensure that people continue to develop their creativity.

In previous chapters, we described how to apply creative intelligence in a business innovation journey. In the final chapter, LEAD, we'll argue that getting serious about creativity also requires a redesign of your board.

Reflection

Having read through this eighth principle, take a moment to consider the following questions:

- Do you make use of the charm of three in strategy development?
- What are the key shifts for your business transformation?
- Is your company organized for ongoing exploration?

LEAD
Redesign Your Board

"Tomorrow belongs to those that prepare for it today."

Malcolm X.[1]

Apply whole-brain thinking

In this chapter, we will explain the importance of creating a whole-brain board for your business. By doing this, you will have the leadership characteristics needed to create the future direction of your business. We will explore the changing role of the board and how to create a board that responds effectively and leads the organization through business transformation smoothly.

A new business direction often calls for board renewal. Sometimes this can be achieved through learning new knowledge and skills, which we encourage directors to spend more time on. The quote from Malcolm X above is the second half of a sentence. In the first half, he stresses the importance of learning, saying that education is the passport for the future and indicating that this is the way to prepare for tomorrow. We couldn't agree more. However, there are times when boardroom education is not enough, and you will need to change the composition of the board to prepare for a new future.

Puma survived after almost going bankrupt in the early 1990s thanks to the then new CEO, Jochen Zeitz, who successfully transformed Puma from sport to fashion.[2] In his own words:

> "We decided that sports, lifestyle and fashion were three elements that could be mixed together to a very unique formula. That's what we did: make Puma a sports-fashion

brand when, at the time, everybody talked about sports performance and functionality." [3]

Puma was the first sports company to work with fashion designers such as Jil Sander and Alexander McQueen. Zeitz also appointed new board members to support Puma's transformation, adding right-brain skills such as empathy (understanding consumer behavior) and creativity (fashion design). In 2007, more than ten years later, the majority of the Puma shares was bought by Kering, the fashion group including Gucci, Saint Laurent and Balenciaga. In 2010, Zeitz became the Chief Sustainability Officer (CSO) of Kering, and later Chairman of the Board's sustainable development committee.

We find it interesting to look at new board appointments from a strategic direction perspective to understand where the business is heading. Continuing with the Kering story, they sold their Puma shares in 2018 and appointed three new board members in 2021: actress Emma Watson, former CEO of Credit Suisse Tidjane Thiam and tech entrepreneur Jean Liu. [4] At a first glance it looks like they value diversity, and once you understand actress Emma Watson is also an activist and a strong advocate for sustainable fashion her appointment as the new chair of the sustainability committee makes sense. Since fashion is one of the most polluting industries in the world, we hope they will take a more active role in changing the rules of the game.

Does your board reflect your future direction? Making sure you have the expertise in your board that supports your business direction sounds obvious but is not yet a business reality. In the Netherlands, for example, the yearly Board Benchmark by Aalt Klaassen [5] shows that traditional left-brain competences such as financial expertise, administrative experience and legal expertise are still the dominant selection criteria when appointing new board members. However, in the same research, board members conclude they need to improve their digital, marketing and HR expertise. There are other signals that boardroom compositions are slowly changing, like the fact that both of us with our design backgrounds have been asked to join boards. More and more boards are aiming for diversity both in expertise and ways of thinking. The question is whether those board changes are fast enough to keep up with the rate of change in the outside world.

The Puma example comes from the article "Fundamental strategy changes for board members: please not on my watch" by Professor Fred Eenennaam and Ruth Soesman. In it, they introduce the metaphor of a rocky landscape. The executive team climbs one rock, but the landscape is changing. Will they keep competing on the current rock, find a new rock, create a new rock or even change the underlying landscape? It's a fundamental question. The supervisory board is a key sparring partner for the leadership team in this process, and in the end approves the decision. Supervisory boards tend to be risk-averse and biased to stay on the same rock. Both of us have experienced that the governance of a business requires a different board composition, different board dynamics and more time investment during a period of fundamental strategy change than during settled ongoing business. Accelerated change means that companies will regularly face strategic redesigns, and this means a left-brain dominant board that only focuses on risk management is not enough. Companies need whole-brain boards that balance managing opportunities and risks.

Boards that lead

Whether to stay climbing the same rock or not is a fundamental question that belongs in the boardroom. Traditionally, this would be the responsibility of the executive board, with supervisory boards acting more in the background. In modern governance, the focus is on creating long-term value for the enterprise with a general agreement that this requires a more active role from the supervisory board. There's an ongoing debate on what being active should look like. Some say you should not "sit on the CEO's chair," but we feel this argument muddles the conversation because it's possible to become more active without taking over the executive role. For us, having an independent mindset and being clear about what role you take at what moment are key characteristics of non-executive directors. Are you acting as the supervisor, the sparring partner, the employer or the ambassador?

We believe in a shared leadership model for executive and non-executive directors, as is also advocated by Ram Charan, Dennis Carey and Michael Useem in their book **Boards That Lead: When to take charge, when to partner, and when to stay out of the way.**[6] They invite directors to shift their role from being a "monitor" to being a "leader." They argue that the gap between the poorly run boards and the well-run boards is caused by human dynamics, and they call for increased board engagement and collaborative leadership. Directors should focus on fundamental topics such as defining the purpose and values (see CARE), ensuring the right leadership team is in place and successors are identified (see ENGAGE), setting a high bar on ethics and risk, and safeguarding constructive boardroom dynamics.

This takes us back to Ludo Van der Heyden's five Cs of fair play that we described in Chapter 5: ACT.[7] Directors should lead by example and inspire the rest of the company.

Bringing the five Cs to life in the boardroom means:

- **Consistency**: ensuring that all people are treated equally and have the same information
- **Clarity**: being transparent about your intentions and putting the real issues on the table
- **Communication**: collecting insights from – and exchanging ideas with –your relevant stakeholders
- **Changeability**: being willing and able to change your opinion and direction when obtaining new insights

- **Culture**: having a shared commitment to the purpose and values of the company and the openness to evaluate and learn

The five Cs are the foundation for ensuring constructive dynamics and meaningful, value-adding dialogues in the boardroom. This is a joint responsibility of the non-executive and the executive directors. In fact, board engagement is one of the six mindsets that distinguishes excellent CEOs from the rest, according to **CEO Excellence**.[8] To build and maintain trust, the best CEOs dare to be transparent in their boards and develop a strong relationship with the chair. They also encourage the board to renew itself, ensuring onboarding and organizing continuous learning. Lastly, they promote a forward-looking agenda.

Changing the agenda is a low hanging fruit when it comes to realizing board transformation. As a CEO told us:

> "Presenting to my Supervisory Board always felt like a chore. The meetings failed to inspire me, which is a pity when you see the profiles of my board members and imagine what they could bring to the table. I never thought of the agenda as a tool to facilitate better dialogues, but now that I do, I really benefit from their different perspectives."

Board engagement requires the right-brain creative and social skills we described in Chapter 4: LEARN, which also explains our own role in boards. You need to design your board's role, composition and learning program to fit your company and its environment. Accelerated change and business innovation should also transform boards. We stimulate the companies we partner with to evaluate the design of their board regularly and have the courage to let go of common practices such as automatic renewal of board terms when needed. We see that many board composition evaluations focus on the type of expertise needed (i.e., Digital Transformation, HR, Finance, Legal) and the diversity in gender, age and race that is wanted. We encourage you to embrace a broader concept of diversity and include the thinking styles, attitudes and skills of the whole-brain approach. When we facilitate discussions on the redesign of boards, we include a section on characteristics in the traditional board composition matrix, keeping in mind that we strive for a mix of gender, age and race.

WHAT IS THE IDEAL BOARD COMPOSITION FOR YOUR COMPANY?

BOARD MEMBERS	A	B	C	D	E	F	G	H
Areas of experience and expertise								
Industry								
Finance and risk								
Sales and marketing								
Legal								
Strategy								
Sustainability								
Technology/IT/digitization								
Organization and operation								
Innovation								
HR, leadership and culture								
Governance								
Key characteristics								
Entrepreneurial spirit								
Future orientation								
Providing wisdom								
Keeping calm under stress								
Challenging conventions								
Ensure open communication								
Analytical and critical reasoning								
People centric								
Fair process								
International perspectives								

This is an example of a board composition matrix we use to map the current and the desired situation in the boards we partner with.

Sensing, pivoting and aligning

Seeing the world from the perspective of the boardroom puts you at risk of living in a bubble. It takes a conscious effort to stay in touch with the undercurrents of society, emerging trends, and the needs of your customers and employees. This is where the observation skills that are part of creative intelligence can make a difference. We like the quote by Marcel Proust that expresses this, "The real voyage of discovery consists not in seeking new landscapes but in having new eyes."[9]

To identify opportunities for innovation by sensing what is going on in your environment, you need to be open to other points of view and be in dialogue with people from different walks of life. One way to do this is by networking with people outside your immediate circle, as we explained in LEARN. The article[10] "Innovation and corporate renewal also disrupts board" describes many other ways, and was written by Liselotte Engstam, together with the Royal Institute of Technology and INSEAD. Liselotte is a thought leading Swedish Non-Executive Director and fellow INSEAD IDP-C who initiated the Digoshen[11] international innovation and impact network that we take part in. Her research objective was to explore how boards can strategically address innovation challenges in more effective ways. The research identified three competences that boards need to create suitable conditions for corporate renewal: sensing, pivoting and aligning.[11] We use this article with boards as a starting point for a dialogue on how to improve those competencies.

Sensing refers to the competency that enables you to connect with and develop new insights into the company's external environment. According to McKinsey research, 84% of board directors lack strong understanding of the dynamics of their firms industries, which makes this a key competency to develop. It requires directors to spend less time reviewing internal materials and more time tapping into outside sources. Traditionally, this is done by inviting experts to board meetings to deep dive into new technologies, business models or other topics. Seldom do boards speak to customers directly. Liselotte Engstam is a great advocate for this. She told us in one of our conversations:

> "We should spend more time looking outwards. Engaging with customers stimulates the board's customer orientation, and in the end will improve the performance."

We encourage boards to ask themselves how far they want to look ahead, what is their horizon for long-term value creation? Which role do they want to play in their industry? Is their company an innovator or a part of the late majority on Rogers' adoption curve?[12] Which trends are relevant for them, and what are they doing today to identify those trends? We recommend boards engage with young talents and build an innovation ecosystem with start-ups, knowledge institutions and other actors. Interacting with the founders of start-ups, who often have an uncanny feeling for the future, is a fast and fun way to keep up to date.

WHERE DOES YOUR COMPANY WANT TO BE ON THE INNOVATION ADOPTION CURVE?

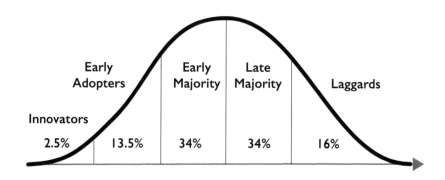

The innovation adoption curve was developed by Rogers[12] for consumers but can also be used for companies. Your desired place on the curve also determines which trends are relevant for you to follow.

Pivoting refers to the competency to use the insights to adjust, or newly create, the company's business model, offer and/or organization, culture and leadership. Boards should question if their purpose gives direction and if their company has the innovation culture and learning mindset described in Chapter 3: CARE and Chapter 4: LEARN. We also recommend working with an innovation subcommittee (beyond the audit and renumeration ones that are most common) and changing the board agenda to focus more time on future challenges and opportunities.

Lastly, aligning refers to the competency to ensure agile decision-making and resource allocation, turning the pivots into a new reality both inside the corporation and for the customer. Aligning is the bridge between strategy and execution. The change manager at the educational institution we partnered with used the metaphor of theater: the script has been written, but the actors are free to do their own interpretation and experiment. We worked together with Sandra Boer of Art Partner, a consultancy that specializes in connecting organizations with artists who bring fresh perspectives and can be a catalyst for change. Sandra Boer told us she brought in theater makers and visual artists and curated a program to develop more ownership of the vision, and to make visible what was invisible:

> "This is really about trust. I remember the CEO saying when he hired us, 'So I don't know what's going to happen, you tell me it's going to create friction for sure, I don't know where we'll end up, and still you expect me to say yes to this?' And I told him he was basically right, the only thing we could offer him for sure was a whole different kind of attention from the artists. And probably a different energy level and dialogue. To say yes to that kind of adventure requires personal courage."

Boards need to ensure that strategy development and execution is organized as a change management process as explained in Chapter 5: ACT, and sponsor experiments as described in Chapter 8: EXPLORE.

Create an innovation board

The changing role of the board means a greater demand on non-executive directors. Beyond monitoring the work of the executive board, they should develop foresight, safeguard an innovation culture and collectively lead the company. Additionally, they need to increase diversity, improve boardroom dynamics and stimulate boardroom learning. This means a greater time investment for board members. For most non-executive directors, it is a part-time role making this a challenge. This is especially true for those who have an executive role in another company. Even when all agree that "create what is not yet" should be a larger part of the agenda, the traditional financial and legal monitoring tasks required by law can consume all the time available. Besides, many people with the right-brain mindsets and skills required for business innovation are not very motivated by left-brain dominated monitoring tasks. Therefore, we encourage CEOs to set up an innovation board, either as a subcommittee of the supervisory board or as a separate advisory board. Just as the audit committee increases the quality of financial responsibility, the innovation board stimulates future thinking and innovation.

Two of our favorite regions in Europe are Italy and Scandinavia. Both have strong design heritages and innovation practices that you can learn from when designing these types of boards. Sweden, Finland and Denmark are consistently in the top ten of most innovative countries in the world (as is our own nation, the Netherlands),[13] and Stockholm and Amsterdam are both in the top ten biggest start-up hubs in Europe.[14] We regularly see Nordic companies work with future-oriented board committees, although they may have different names and objectives to fit their business needs. Danish Novo Nordisk, for example, has an R&D board committee, while Swedish Essity has a portfolio development committee and Dutch Ahold has a sustainability and innovation board committee. Nordic boards also often see sustainability as an opportunity for innovation, rather than managing it for compliance. Take Maersk, a 118-year-old Danish global logistics company that is leading the way in sustainable business models for the shipping industry.[15] They have pledged to launch the first carbon-neutral containership by 2023. Maersk is also an example of the shared leadership model for executives and non-executives that we described earlier. Jim Hagemann Snabe, Chair of the Board, describes their role in the transformation of Maersk as follows:

> "The role of the board is changing. It needs to help executives formulate a compelling and relevant dream and then create the conditions that allow executives to experiment and not be constrained by too many details. The board's focus has to shift towards the future rather than the past."

We enjoy Italy because of its strong cultural heritage combined with entrepreneurship, which comes with an appreciation for craftsmanship, quality and improvisation. Italy is the benchmark for entrepreneurial leaders partnering with creative people, and Milan is a top ten start-up hub. Business families play an important role in these creative partnerships. Like in other European countries, about 85% of Italian businesses are family owned,[16] but, in Italy, two out of three are managed by family members (compared to one out of ten in the United Kingdom for example). Another key difference is their longevity. Five out of the top ten oldest businesses in the world are Italian, including the Venetian glass company Barovier & Toso that was established in 1295. The design and manufacturing of luxury goods such as Murano glass, fashion and furniture is what Italy is famous for. For these types of companies, working with designers is part of their core business.

An intuitive connection based on their right-brain dominance, shared purpose and values is the recipe for their success.

Natuzzi, Italy's largest furniture house that was founded in 1959 by Pasquale Natuzzi and has been listed on the New York Stock Exchange since 1993, is an example of this.[17] One of the Natuzzi values is sustainability, which they poetically describe as "loving and respecting nature, starting with the raw materials that our artisans lovingly handle day by day."[18] And like our Nordic board examples, Pasquale Natuzzi sees sustainability as an opportunity, "Our commitment for sustainable development is not only a responsibility, but also an opportunity."

Natuzzi is present in 123 countries across five continents, and their creative partnerships also have a global reach. Dutch Designer Borre Akkersdijk, Co-Founder of textile innovation company BYBORRE, is one of Natuzzi's creative partners. He told Anne Mieke, who is the Chair of his Board of Directors, how he was inspired by the Natuzzi family's values:

> "The first thing Pasquale, Jr., Natuzzi's Creative Director, said to me was that if we were going to work together, I needed to understand the heart and soul of their home in Puglia. The Natuzzi family is deeply connected to the surrounding nature, the soil and the sea. By thinking about the future of people and the planet, we are finding new ways to create quality, custom and sustainable fabrics."

When Fennemiek studied design direction at the Domus Academy in Milan in 1990, she first realized how inspiring it was to work with Italian business entrepreneurs such as Alessandro Alessi. He partnered with designers and architects such as Alessandro Mendini not only to design products but also to design the future direction of his company. In the north of Europe, it is unusual to see business leaders rely on the sensing and creating qualities of creatives for strategy development. The reason why it is more common in Italy is partly because many Italian companies are design-driven, such as Natuzzi. But it goes beyond that. It is also rooted in the common appreciation of art and culture in Italian society. Entrepreneurs in other Italian industries also believe in the interplay between the worlds of culture and business. Adriano Olivetti's vision for the computer company Olivetti was inspired by his partnerships with scholars, sociologists, artists and philosophers.[19] Stefano Marzano, Fennemiek's professor at the Domus Academy and later Head of Design at Philips, helped create the Philips Vision of the Future.[20] This vision led to the design of a Simplicity Advisory Board to provide ongoing perspectives into how simplicity could be better implemented throughout the entire company.[21] Following the Italian tradition, the first Simplicity Board included a fashion designer, architect, radiology experience expert, IT professor and art teacher.

What would your ideal innovation board look like? We encourage you to set up a team of "outside the box" thinkers from uncommon backgrounds to inspire the leadership team and unleash the creativity that is needed to design the future of your business.

This is where our story about creativity in business ends. In Part One, we wrote about why it's time to get serious about creativity. In Part Two, we encouraged you to start learning by doing, and, in Part Three, we showed you how to design the future of your business and your board.

Are you ready to start your own business innovation journey?

Summary

In this chapter, we discussed how you can ensure you have the mindsets and skills you need on your board by taking a whole-brain approach to its membership. With the changing role of the board, we explained how to ensure that the board responds positively to this change by allowing more time on the agenda to explore the future and developing the board's right-brain orientation through stimulating boardroom learning, inviting new board members or installing innovation subcommittees. We've shown how Scandinavian and Italian businesses can be a source of inspiration for this.

Reflection

Having read through this ninth principle, take a moment to consider the following questions:

- Is your board designed to be future-proof?
- How could they add more value in the business innovation journey?
- Do you see a role for an innovation board in your company?

APPLY
Conclusion

"Everyone thinks of changing the world,
but no one thinks of changing himself."

Leo Tolstoy[1]

Lead by example

Do you want to design a better future for your business? And are you open to change your own approach as Tolstoy encourages you to do?

Re-inventing your business starts with re-inventing your own way of working and that of the board of directors. To return to the Introduction, we believe that leaders who embrace their creativity can change their business for the better. When it's time for business renewal, adjust the way you usually develop your strategy and design the future of your business as you would design any new product.

In this fast-changing world, you cannot wait until it's time to design a second business curve. You need to be in a state of permanent beta. Above all, this requires you to adopt a growth mindset and create a learning culture in your whole organization. Beyond the focus on continuous improvement, you also need to be prepared for potential disruption and fundamental business transformation by organizing regular "what if?" sessions and innovation labs.

Experiment with our creative principles

We hope you have enjoyed reading our book and will also enjoy experimenting with applying the nine guiding principles of our creative approach in your own business. To summarize, the nine principles are as follows:

1. **CREATE**: Let's get serious about creativity. Creating your future direction is a design challenge. Encourage your team to think and act as a designer in a business context. Creativity matters for future business success.

2. **CHANGE**: It's time to transform. Accelerated change calls for business transformation. Think about how you can take the lead in realizing societal change. The need for sustainability is an opportunity to change your business for the better.

3. **CARE**: Embrace your purpose. Purpose gives direction. Building an innovation culture starts with caring to do better. Identify the shared purpose and values of your organization to accelerate transformation.

4. **LEARN**: Build your creative confidence. Applying whole-brain thinking can change business for the better. Creativity can be learned. Design and implement learning programs that encourage your team to embrace their creative intelligence.

5. **ACT**: Learn by doing. Design processes are iterative: generate ideas, select the most promising ones, learn from prototyping and keep on improving. Dare to learn by doing and always ask yourself: how could I do this better?

6. **ENGAGE**: Involve and empower people. People make the difference between an average result and a great one. Diversity makes teams better. Combine insiders with outsiders, big-picture perspectives with niche expertise and unusual thinkers with creative makers.

7. **ENVISION**: Imagine a better future. Business innovation starts with imagining a better future. What does good look like? First create a shared vision of your desired destination so that you can then design the road to get there.

8. **EXPLORE**: Make it happen. Dream big, start small. Adapt a designer's mindset. Be curious about the world around you, look

for new opportunities and use experiments to learn and keep moving in the right direction.

9. **LEAD**: Redesign your board. New business directions call for new competencies. Design boardroom learning programs and a forward-looking agenda. Consider creating an additional innovation board to stimulate future thinking and innovation.

Be kind to yourself

Acknowledge that it's difficult to be creative and have an open mind to reflect on the future of your business when you're busy managing your ongoing business. Should you change your personal exploit/explore balance? Are you making sure you fill your own creativity well? Remember, your creative muscle needs nourishment, so allow yourself time off to talk to people, go to museums, learn new things, read, play, or whatever else you enjoy that stimulates your curiosity and your senses.

You may also like our *Creativity Matters* newsletter, in which we share our sources of inspiration, insights from our work with clients and interviews with innovation leaders. You can sign up for it via our website: www.caracta.com/creativity-matters.

Stay in touch

We believe that, when implemented, the principles of our approach will make your business future fit and would love to hear about your experiences applying them in your own business. Learning about what worked for you, and what didn't, helps us improve the innovation journeys and learning programs we design for our clients.

If you have any suggestions for items in our newsletter, companies we can learn from, books that may inspire us or if you're curious to find out more about us, please email us on info@caracta.com.

References

ENJOY: Introduction

1. Carnegie, D, *How to Win Friends and Influence People*, 100th anniversary edition (Simon & Schuster, 2010)

2. Buckminster Fuller, R, and López-Pérez, D, *R. Buckminster Fuller: Pattern-thinking* (Lars Müller Publishers, 2019)

3. Frost, R, *The Poetry of Robert Frost: The collected poems* (Holt Paperbacks, 2002)

4. Newton, I, "Isaac Newton letter to Robert Hooke" (5 February 1675), Historical Society of Pennsylvania Simon Gratz autograph collection (#0250A), Box 12/11, Folder 37.

PART ONE: THE FOUNDATION

1. CREATE: Innovation Is A Design Challenge

1. Nordstrom, K, and Ridderstrale, J, *Karaoke Capitalism: Managing for mankind* (Pearson Education Canada, 2003)

2. Kahn, CH, and Heraclitus, *The Art and Thought of Heraclitus* (Cambridge University Press, 1981)

3. ScaleUpNation, "Art of scaling: Research on ambidextrous leadership" (2022), https://scaleupnation.com/the-art-of-scaling, accessed 19 October 2022

4. DXC Technology, "Digital transformation is racing ahead, and no business is immune", *Harvard Business Review* (19 July 2017), https://hbr.org/sponsored/2017/07/digital-transformation-is-racing-ahead-and-no-industry-is-immune-2, accessed 19 October 2022

5. Roser, M, Ortiz-Ospina, E, and Ritchie, H, "Life expectancy", Our World in Data (2013), https://ourworldindata.org/life-expectancy

6. Handy, C, *The Second Curve: Thoughts on reinventing society* (Random House Business, 2015)

7. Browne, J, *Darwin's Origins of Species: A biography* (Atlantic Monthly Press, 2007)

8. Surowiecki, J, "Where Nokia went wrong", *The New Yorker* (3 September 2013), www.newyorker.com/business/currency/where-nokia-went-wrong

9. Mui, C, "How Kodak failed", *Forbes* (18 January 2012), www.forbes.com/sites/chunkamui/2012/01/18/how-kodak-failed, accessed 19 October 2022

10. Catmull, E, and Wallace, A, *Creativity, Inc.: Overcoming the unseen forces that stand in the way of true inspiration* (Random House, 2014)

11. World Economic Forum, *The Future of Jobs Report 2020* (20 October 2020) www.weforum.org/reports/the-future-of-jobs-report-2020

12. IBM, *Global CEO Study* (2010, 2012) [Over 1,500 corporate heads and public sector leaders across 60 nations and 33 industries polled]

13. Prior, J, "Creativity has become the elephant in the board room", *The Huffington Post* (3 January 2012), www.huffingtonpost.co.uk/jim-prior/creativity-has-become-the_b_1180607.html

2. CHANGE: It's Time To Transform

1. "The Times They Are A-Changin'" is a song written by Bob Dylan and released as the title track of his 1964 album of the same name.

2. Schwab, K, "The Fourth Industrial Revolution: What it means, how to respond" (14 January 2016), www.weforum.org/agenda/2016/01/the-fourth-industrial-revolution-what-it-means-and-how-to-respond, accessed 19 October 2022

3. Xu, X, Lu, Y, Vogel-Heuser, B, and Wang, L, "Industry 4.0 and Industry 5.0: Inception, conception and perception", *Journal of Manufacturing Systems*, 61 (October 2021), www.researchgate.net/publication/355391185_Industry_40_and_Industry_50-Inception_conception_and_perception, accessed 19 October 2022

4. Keen, A, *How to Fix the Future: Staying human in a digital age* (Atlantic Books, 2018)

5. Leonhard, G, *Technology vs Humanity: The coming clash between man and machine* (Futures Agency, 2019)

6. Meadows, DH, Meadows, DL, Randers, J, and Behrens III, WW, *The Limits to Growth* (Universe Books, 1972)

7. Edelman, "Edelman Trust Barometer" (2021), www.edelman.com/trust/2021-trust-barometer, accessed 19 October 2022

8. Marcario, R, "Quotes", Business of Purpose (2020), www.businessofpurpose.com/quotes, accessed 19 October 2022

9. Rittel, HWJ, and Webber, MM, "Dilemmas in a general theory of planning", *Policy Science*, 4 (1973), https://link.springer.com/article/10.1007/BF01405730, accessed 19 October 2022

10. Camillus, JC, "Strategy as a wicked problem", *Harvard Business Review* (May 2008), https://hbr.org/2008/05/strategy-as-a-wicked-problem, accessed 19 October 2022

11. Ayres, C, "Revenge is best served cold – on YouTube: How a broken guitar became a smash hit", *The Sunday Times* (22 July 2009), www.thetimes.co.uk/article/revenge-is-best-served-cold-on-youtube-2dhbsh6jtp5, accessed 19 October 2022

12. Bentley, JC, "Wicked or tame?", Taming Wicked Problems (11 July 2014), http://tamingwickedproblems.com/wicked-or-tame, accessed 19 October 2022

13. Vermaak, H, *Plezier beleven aan taaie vraagstukken* (Kluwer, 2009)

14. Albert, M, *Capitalism vs. Capitalism* (Whurr Publishers, 1993)

15. Bezemer, PJ, *Diffusion of Corporate Governance Beliefs*, Rotterdam School of Management, Ph.D. thesis (19 March 2010), https://repub.eur.nl/pub/18458, accessed 19 October 2022

16. Davis, I, and Dickson, T, "Lou Gerstner on corporate reinvention and values", *McKinsey Quarterly* (1 September 2014),

www.mckinsey.com/featured-insights/leadership/lou-gerstner-on-corporate-reinvention-and-values, accessed 19 October 2022

17. Boynton, A, "Unilever's Paul Polman: CEOs can't be 'slaves' to shareholders", *Forbes* (20 July 2015), www.forbes.com/sites/andyboynton/2015/07/20/unilevers-paul-polman-ceos-cant-be-slaves-to-shareholders, accessed 19 October 2022

18. Atkins, B, "Demystifying ESG: Its history & current status", *Forbes* (8 June 2020) www.forbes.com/sites/betsyatkins/2020/06/08/demystifying-esgits-history--current-status/?sh=71b2461c2cdd, accessed 19 October 2022

3. CARE: Embrace Your True Purpose

1. Vagianos, A, "Ruth Bader Ginsburg tells young women: 'Fight for the things you care about'", *The Huffington Post* (2 June 2015), www.huffingtonpost.co.uk/entry/ruth-bader-ginsburg-fight-for-the-things-you-care-about_n_7492630, accessed 19 October 2022

2. Ashkenas, R, "We still don't know the difference between change and transformation", *Harvard Business Review* (15 January 2015), https://hbr.org/2015/01/we-still-dont-know-the-difference-between-change-and-transformation, accessed 19 October 2022

3. Kotter, J, *Leading Change* (Harvard Business Review Press, 2012)

4. Monefiore, SS, *Speeches That Changed the World* (Quercus, 2020)

5. EY Beacon Institute and Harvard Business Review Analytic Services, *The Business Case for Purpose* (Harvard Business School Publishing, 2015)

6. Hill, L, *Collective Genius: The art and practice of leading innovation* (Harvard Business Review Press, 2014)

7. Aziz, A, "The power of purpose: The business case for purpose (All The Data You Were Looking For Pt 2)", *Forbes* (7 March 2020), www.forbes.com/sites/afdhelaziz/2020/03/07/

the-power-of-purpose-the-business-case-for-purpose-all-the-data-you-were-looking-for-pt-2, accessed 19 October 2022

8. Mourkogiannis, N, *Purpose: The starting point of great companies* (Palgrave Macmillan, 2008)

9. Sinek, S, "How great leaders inspire action", TED Talk (2009), www.ted.com/talks/simon_sinek_how_great_leaders_inspire_action, accessed 19 October 2022

10. Kapferer, J, *The New Strategic Brand Management* (Kogan Page, 1997)

11. Aaker, David A, and Joachimsthaler, E, *Brand Leadership* (Free Press Business, 2000)

12. Profitable Venture, "50 business quotes & words of wisdom from great entrepreneurs" (2014), www.profitableventure.com/entrepreneurial-quotes, accessed 19 October 2022

4. LEARN: Build Your Creative Confidence

1. Einstein, A, and Calaprice, A, *The Ultimate Quotable Einstein* (Princeton University Press, 2010)

2. Furr, N, Innovation in the Age of Disruption (INSEAD course, 2020), www.insead.edu/executive-education/online-innovation-programmes

3. Dweck, C, *Growth Mindset: Changing the way you think to fulfil your potential* (Little, Brown Book Group, 2017)

4. Reeves, M, Faeste, L, Whitaker, K, and Hassan, F, "The truth about corporate Transformation", *MIT Sloan Management Review* (31 January 2018), https://sloanreview.mit.edu/article/the-truth-about-corporate-transformation, accessed 19 October 2022

5. Hoffer, E, *The Ordeal of Change* (Hopewell Publications, 2006)

6. Herrmann, N, *The Whole Brain Business Book* (McGraw-Hill, 1996)

7. Burkes, D, *The Myths of Creativity* (Jossey-Bass, 2014)

8. Beahm, G, I, *Steve: Steve Jobs in his own words* (Agate B2, 2011)

9. Robinson, K, "Do schools kill creativity?", TED Talk (2006), www.ted.com/talks/sir_ken_robinson_do_schools_kill_creativity, accessed 19 October 2022

10. Brown, B, *Daring Greatly: How the courage to be vulnerable transforms the way we live, love, parent, and lead* (Penguin Books, 2015)

11. Smith, P, *You Can Find Inspiration in Everything (*And if You Can't, Look Again!)* (Violette Editions, 2001)

PART 2: THE BRIDGE

5. ACT: Learn By Doing

1. Earhart, A. (1935). https://ameliaearhart.com/quotes, accessed 19 October 2022

2. Tichy, N, and Charan, R, "Speed, simplicity, self-confidence: An interview with Jack Welch", *Harvard Business Review* (September–October 1989), https://hbr.org/1989/09/speed-simplicity-self-confidence-an-interview-with-jack-welch, accessed 19 October 2022

3. Ibarra, H, and Obodaru, O, "Women and the vision thing", *Harvard Business Review Magazine* (January 2009), https://hbr.org/2009/01/women-and-the-vision-thing, accessed 19 October 2022

4. Ryan, KJ, "Richard Branson on why he rarely says no". *Inc.* (19 April 2016), www.inc.com, accessed 19 October 2022

5. Kerr, SP, et al., "Risk attitudes and personality traits of entrepreneurs and venture team members", *Proceedings of the National Academy of Sciences of the United States of America* (19 August 2019), www.pnas.org/doi/10.1073/pnas.1908375116, accessed 19 October 2022

6. Ries, E, *The Lean StartUp: How today's entrepreneurs use continuous innovation to create radically successful businesses* (Random House USA, 2017)

7. Franken, RE, *Human Motivation* (Brooks/Cole Publishing Company, 1993)

8. Michalko, M, *ThinkerToys: A handbook of creative-thinking techniques* (Ten Speed Press, 1991)

9. Osborn, AF, *How to Think Up* (McGraw-Hill, 1942)

10. Csikszentmihalyi, M, *Creativity: Flow and the psychology of discovery and invention* (Harper Perennial, 1996)

11. Van der Heyden, L, "Business compliance: Setting a tone of fairness a the top", Baltzer Science Publishers (May 2013), www.ludovanderheyden.com/blog/setting-a-tone-of-fairness-at-the-top-business-compliance, accessed 19 October 2022

PART 3: THE PRACTICE

6. ENGAGE: Involve And Empower People

1. Brown, B, "The Power of vulnerability", TED Talk (2020), www.ted.com/talks/brene_brown_the_power_of_vulnerability, accessed 19 October 2022

2. Von Der Linn, B, "Overview of GE's change acceleration process CAP", *Agility Science* (25 January 2009), https://bvonderlinn. wordpress.com/2009/01/25/overview-of-ges-change-acceleration-process-cap, accessed 19 October 2022

3. Mendelow, AL, "Environmental scanning: The impact of the stakeholder concept", from *Proceedings From the Second International Conference on Information Systems*, (Association for Computing Machinery, 1981), pp407–418

4. Walsh, C, "On building a faster horse: Design thinking for disruption", *Forbes* (19 October 2017), www.forbes.com/sites/forbesfinancecouncil/2017/10/19/on-building-a-faster-horse-design-thinking-for-disruption, accessed 19 October 2022

5. Osterwalder, A, *Value Proposition Design: How to create products and services customers want* (Wiley, 2014)

6. Rombouts, P, for more information on his approach, see https://peterrombouts.com, accessed 19 October 2022

7. Janis, IL, *Victims of Groupthink: A psychological study of foreign-policy decisions and fiascos* (Houghton Mifflin, 1972)

8. Accenture Institute for High Performance, *Growing Ensemble Leaders Survey* (2014)

7. ENVISION: Imagine A Better Future

1. Roosevelt, E, *My Day: The best of Eleanor Roosevelt's acclaimed newspaper columns 1936–1962* (Da Capo Press, 2001)

2. Johnson, M, & Suskewics, J, *Lead From the Future: How to turn visionary thinking into breakthrough growth* (Gildan Media, 2020)

3. Gide, A, *The Counterfeiters* (Alfred A. Knopf, 1927)

4. Chouinard, Y, *Let My People Go Surfing: The education of a reluctant businessman*, 2nd edition (Penguin Books, 2016)

5. Lego (n.d.), "About us", www.lego.com/nl-nl/aboutus/lego-group/the-lego-group-history, accessed 19 October 2022

6. Lindgren, M, and Bandhold, H, *Scenario Planning: The link between future and strategy* (Palgrave Macmillan, 2003)

7. Shell. (n.d.), "What are Shell scenarios?", www.shell.com/energy-and-innovation/the-energy-future/scenarios/what-are-scenarios.html, accessed 19 October 2022

8. del Marmol, T and Feys, B, *PESTLE Analysis: Understand and plan for your business environment* (50Minutes, 2015)

9. Parnes, SJ, *Creative Behavior Guidebook* (Charles Scribners & Sons, 1967)

10. de Bono, E, *Lateral Thinking* (Penguin, 1977)

11. Wardle, D, "'What if?' The secret tool that created Disneyland, Netflix and Uber", *Strive Magazine* (July-Sept 2019 issue), https://magazine.thestriveproject.com/issue/jul-sept-2019/what-if-the-secret-tool-that-created-disneyland-netflix-and-uber, accessed 19 October 2022

12. Dewar, C, Keller, S, and Malhotra, V, *CEO Excellence: The six mindsets that distinguish the best leaders from the rest* (Simon & Schuster, 2022)

13. Ellemers, N, "Bang maken motiveert niet, hoop geven wel", *Het Financieele Dagblad* (13 September 2021) https://fd.nl/opinie/1412020/bang-maken-motiveert-niet-hoop-geven-wel, accessed 19 October 2022

14. de Saint-Exupéry, A, *The Little Prince* (Clarion Books, 2000)

8. EXPLORE: Make It Happen

1. Petras, K, and Petras, R, *It Always Seems Impossible Until It's Done* (Workman Publishing, 2014)

2. Kahneman, D, *Thinking Fast and Slow* (Penguin Books, 2012)

3. van Eck, M, and Leenhouts, E, *The One-Page Business Strategy* (Pearson, 2014), this book explains the OGSM model, which was built on Peter Drucker's ideas and has been around since the 1950s

4. Aslander, M, and Witteveen, E, *Nooit af* (Business Contact, 2015)

5. Attributed to Don Walsh, American oceanographer and explorer

6. Kotter, JP, *Accelerate: Building strategic agility for a faster-moving world* (Harvard Business Review Press, 2014)

7. Neumeier, M, *Metaskills: Five talents for the robotic age* (Addison Wesley, 2012)

9. LEAD: Redesign Your Board

1. X, Malcolm, *By Any Means Necessary* (Pathfinder Books, 1970) [quote from his 28 June 1964 speech at the Founding Rally of the Organization of Afro-American Unity]

2. Eenennaam, F, and Soesman, R, "Fundamentele strategieverandering voor commissarissen: Please not on my watch", *Journal of Interactive Marketing* (2008), 257–274

3. Zeitz, J. "Transcript PUMA CEO and Chairman Jochen Zeitz", CNN World Business (28 September 2006), http://edition.cnn.com/2006/BUSINESS/07/06/boardroom.zeitz, accessed 19 October 2022

4. Kering press release, "Jean Liu, Tidjane Thiam and Emma Watson join the board of Kering as directors", (16 June 2020), www.kering.com/en/news/jean-liu-tidjane-thiam-and-emma-watson-join-the-board-of-kering-as-directors, accessed 19 October 2022

5. Klaassen, A, "Commissarissen benchmarkonderzoek 2017–2018 – Deel II", Grant Thornton (February 2018), https://www.grantthornton.nl/globalassets/1.-member-firms/netherlands/insights/thema/commissarissenonderzoek/2018/commissarissen-benchmarkonderzoek---2017-2018-deel-ii---grant-thornton.pdf, accessed 19 October 2022

6. Charan, R, Carey, D, and Useem, M, *Boards That Lead: When to take charge, when to partner, and when to stay out of the way* (Harvard Business Review Press, 2014)

7. Van der Heyden, L, "Business compliance: Setting a tone of fairness at the top", Baltzer Science Publishers (May 2013), www.ludovanderheyden.com/blog/setting-a-tone-of-fairness-at-the-top-business-compliance, accessed 19 October 2022

8. Dewar, C, Keller, S, and Malhotra, V, *CEO Excellence: The six mindsets that distinguish the best leaders from the rest* (Simon & Schuster, 2022)

9. Proust, M, *La Prisonnière: À la recherche du temps perdu, vol. V* (Grasset, 1923)

10. Engstam, L, Magnusson, M, van der Heyden, L, and Karlsson, M, "Innovation and corporate renewal also disrupts boards", MGMT of Innovation and Technology (2 June 2019), www.insead.edu/sites/default/files/assets/dept/centres/icgc/docs/innovation-and-corporate-renewal-article.pdf, accessed 19 October 2022

11. Digoshen. (n.d.), "Team Digoshen", https://digoshen.com/team-digoshen, accessed 19 October 2022

12. Rogers, EM, *Diffusion of Innovations* (The Free Press, 2003)

13. Dutta, S, Lanvin, B, Rivera León, L and Wunsch-Vincent, S, "Global Innovation Index 2021", World Intellectual Property Organization (2021), www.wipo.int/edocs/pubdocs/en/wipo_pub_gii_2021.pdf, accessed 19 October 2022

14. Ohr, T, "Top 30: Europe's biggest startup hubs in 2020", EU-Startups (24 November 2020), www.eu-startups.com/2020/11/top-30-europes-biggest-startup-hubs-in-2020, accessed 19 October 2022

15. Shekshnia, S, Buchreitz Jensen, S, and Engstam, L, "What the World Can Learn From Nordic Boards", *INSEAD Knowledge* (1 June 2022), https://knowledge.insead.edu/leadership-organisations/what-world-can-learn-nordic-boards, accessed 19 October 2022

16. AIDAF, Italian Family Business home page (n.d.), www.aidaf.it/en, accessed 19 October 2022

17. Natuzzi Group (n.d.), "Company profile", www.natuzzigroup.com/en-EN/company-profile.html, accessed 19 October 2022

18. Natuzzi Group (n.d.), "Meet Natuzzi", www.natuzzi.com/us/en/meet-natuzzi, accessed 19 October 2022

19. Olivetti, FA, "Adriana Olivetti: A twentieth-century entrepreneur and innovator", https://artsandculture.google.com/story/mwUhh8o5e-foJA, accessed 19 October 2022

20. Philips Design, "Celebrating 90 years of design at Philips" (2015), www.crisprepository.nl/_uploaded/Backgrounder-PhilipsDesign90-years.pdf, accessed 19 October 2022

21. Philips Press Release, "Philips creates simplicity advisory board", *Scoop* (13 December 2004), www.scoop.co.nz/stories/SC0412/S00031/philips-creates-simplicity-advisory-board.htm, accessed 19 October 2022

APPLY: Conclusion

1. 1. Tolstoy, L, *Pamphlets: Translated from the Russian* (Wentworth Press, 2016) [quote from his pamphlet from 1900]

Acknowledgments

This book started to take shape long before the actual publication date. We would never have realized it without the inspiration, patience and feedback of a great many people – all of whom we couldn't possibly thank in this limited space.

Our own creative journeys started when we were children. As Robert Frost's poem states, we took the road less traveled by and it has made all the difference. We're grateful to our parents who let us choose our own paths, even though our entrepreneurial fathers believed this would lead to unemployment. Our mothers were both good with their hands: Fennemiek's mother excelled at gardening and Japanese Ikebana flower arrangements, while Anne Mieke's mother made her own clothes and wished for a future as tailor. She was always positive and kept developing her own talents until she passed away at 90. Fennemiek's father turned 90 years old in 2022 and is another inspiring example of how you can stay curious and keep a growth mindset your whole life.

We are both great believers in lifelong learning and have met some great educators on our way that had a profound impact on our professional lives. People such as architect Andrea Branzi, Cultural Director at the Domus Academy; Ludo Van der Heyden, Professor Corporate Governance at INSEAD; Professor of Arts Education, Ken Robinson: and illustrator and textile designer Akira Minagawa, to name just a few. There have been many others. It's not only professors who have inspired us; other students were equally important to challenging our thinking. Now that we are teaching ourselves, we get new insights from the people in our learning programs. Many of the concepts of this book have been tested first with the students from our Boardroom Oxygen programs, the NCD Governance Essentials course, ScaleUpNation board program and Comenius Global Innovation Leadership course, all of which have improved thanks to their critical questions. Thank you all!

The learning we do through doing and experiencing is equally important to us, and we cherish insights from unusual sources. Co-Directors Ola Mafaalani and Adelheid Roosen's transformational theater, *Women in Bath*, (don't ask…) made us feel the importance of "fun, no matter what" and reminded us to play more. Thanks to them and their fabulous team at Female Economy, the introduction of this book is called ENJOY. Gender equality has been a principle of ours all our lives, but the discussion around feminism and quotas could use some of that lightness as well. We're grateful to Dr. Kaouthar Darmoni, Director of feminist thinktank Atria, for doing just that – and for empowering women through belly dancing. It's so much fun to do and experience your female qualities.

As innovation partners, we enjoy many different business challenges, but what makes a journey truly enjoyable is the company on the road. We appreciate all the great people we've met along the way. In the same way you become a better tennis player when playing against better players, you become a better consultant and board member when partnering with strong clients and colleagues. We've been fortunate to partner with some of the best and used their insights and quotes in this book.

To better understand the wicked challenges companies struggle with, and how creativity can help address those, we wanted input from people beyond our own circle of clients. We're grateful to everyone who introduced us to their relevant academic and business connections, resulting in inspiring trips to the United Kingdom, Silicon Valley, Sweden and Italy. We conducted more than a hundred interviews, met some wonderful people and collected a lot of interesting insights.

In true innovation style, this book is a result of various improvements along the way. We especially want to thank our beta readers, who took the time to read through earlier versions and gave input from different perspectives – from scale-ups to family businesses, from German to Italian, from content to structure. Thank you to Lianne

Bergeron, Chiara Bianchi Dorta, Oscar Kneppers, Kerstin Stranimaier and Lino Tedeschi – without your help, we wouldn't have gotten this far.

Writing a book is not our core business, and we didn't hesitate to involve experts in the process. Our journey started with a workshop by Marja Duin and Linda Krijns, accelerated thanks to *The 30 Day Book Writing Challenge* of Joshua Sprague and continued with input from writing coach Door de Flines. For the final steps, the Rethink Press team was a joy to partner with. We appreciate their help and have learned a lot from working with them.

This list wouldn't be complete without mentioning the people we dedicated this book to: our dearest fellow travelers Frederik Franken, Karst Gommer, Ewout Gommer and Maarten Helle – the most important men in our lives. Without their infinite support, this book wouldn't be here. Their company on our journey is an endless source of joy and inspiration.

The Authors

Fennemiek Gommer

Fennemiek is a purpose-driven strategy and innovation consultant. She complimented her industrial design study with degrees in design thinking, brand strategy

Anne Mieke and Fennemiek

and business in the United States, Italy and France. She enjoys applying her international perspective and design approach to a wide range of business challenges, which is why she ended up as a boardroom consultant. Her specific expertise is in future-led strategy development and connecting people and ideas. Besides being a partner of Caracta Business Innovation, Fennemiek is chair of the board of several family-owned businesses, ambassador for the INSEAD Directors Network and a lecturer in Business Transformation at NCD Governance Essentials.

www.linkedin.com/in/fennemiekgommer

Anne Mieke Eggenkamp

Anne Mieke pioneered digital design surfing on the growth of world wide web and tech developments when she started her own creative studio with a Canadian partner after studying graphic design. Her passion for helping people grow led her to complete a second degree in education and take on her role as chair of the Design Academy Eindhoven. She now acts as an innovation partner, specializing in circularity and sustainability, leadership development and designing board room learning. Besides being a partner of Caracta Business Innovation, Anne Mieke is chair of the board of several scale-up companies, and she lectures about ambidextrous leadership at ScaleUpNation and Comenius.

www.linkedin.com/in/anne-mieke-eggenkamp

Caracta

Caracta Business Innovation is led by Fennemiek Gommer and Anne Mieke Eggenkamp. Working as a duo they believe in the added value of integrating a strategy and leadership development approach to business innovation. They help entrepreneurial leaders apply creativity and work with unconventional experts to design their future direction, brand positioning and transformation journeys.

www.caracta.com